To God, It's Not What You Do...

IT'S
WHO YOU ARE
THAT
COUNTS

DEEPER
devotions

To God, It's Not What You Do...

IT'S
WHO YOU ARE
THAT
COUNTS

Fruit of the Spirit

JAMES LONG

ZondervanPublishingHouse

Grand Rapids, Michigan

A Division of HarperCollinsPublishers

It's Who You Are That Counts
Copyright © 1997 by James Long

Requests for information should be addressed to:

📖 ZondervanPublishingHouse
Grand Rapids, Michigan 49530

Library of Congress Cataloging-in-Publication Data

Long, James, 1949–
   It's who you are that counts / James Long.
      p.   cm.—(Deeper devotions)
   ISBN: 0-310-20601-4 (pbk.)
   1. Fruit of the Spirit. 2. Bible. N.T. Galatians V, 22–23—Devotional
literature. I. Title. II. Series.
BS2685.4.L66   1997
234'.13—DC20   96-46095
                                                                CIP

Interior design by Sue Vandenberg Koppenol

Printed in the United States of America

---

97 98 99 00 01 02 03 04 /❖ DH/ 10 9 8 7 6 5 4 3 2

For my mom,
who reminds me
of Jesus

The fruit of the Spirit is love, joy, peace, patience, kindness, goodness, faithfulness, gentleness and self-control.

—Galatians 5:22–23

Contents

How to use this book

You can simply read it. Front to back. You can read each chapter, complete in one sitting. Or you can skip around, checking out what interests you.

On the other hand, if you want to get the most out of this book, you might try this:

- Read the section marked **"Weekend Reading"** at one sitting when you have a bit more time. Perhaps on Saturday. Or Sunday afternoon. Each "Weekend Reading" section introduces an important theme, and develops it with a true-life story and some thoughts from the Bible. Make that theme your spiritual project for the week, whether the topic is love, patience, self-control. Whatever. There are ten weekly themes in this book.

- Next, take a few minutes each day to remind yourself of the theme, using the one-page **"Daily Checkpoints."** Following each chapter, you will find "Daily Checkpoints," a page a day, marked Monday, Tuesday, Wednesday, Thursday, Friday. You can read these pages and give some thought to the week's theme, even if you have only a few minutes to devote. This will help you develop the habit of setting aside some time each day to think about your faith. You can spend more time, of course. Each day's reading introduces questions, points you to a Bible passage, guides you into a prayer focus. It would be excellent to follow these readings with an open notebook, jotting down insights and questions as you go along.

- It would be helpful several times during the week to take another fresh look at the "Weekend Reading" section. Keep your mind focused on the personal project for the week, the theme of each chapter. You just may find your life changing, little by little, as you remind yourself of the loving concern God has for you.

Acknowledgments

Thanks!

For years, *Campus Life* magazine provided a forum for me to share my ideas and my life. Some of the words in this book first appeared in the magazine, and I am grateful for the permission to reprint them here. Thanks to Harold Smith and my other colleagues at *Campus Life* for their friendship and encouragement. Thanks also to the readers of *Campus Life*, whose letters, comments, and questions further clarified my thinking, and made a significant contribution to this book, and to me.

The manuscript was read and keyboarded by my friend, Marie Gomez, who was, as always, accurate and efficient in her keyboarding; wise and thought-provoking in her observations.

I suppose Harriet, my wife, has read or heard virtually every word I've written for publication. When she makes a suggestion, she has my undivided attention. Experience has taught me that her ideas invariably bring about improvements. This is true in life, as well as in my writing. I am a far better person because of the privilege and joy of knowing her.

My thanks also to you, the reader. It is an endless source of encouragement to me, knowing that after all the years that have come and gone, people like you still trust Jesus, and aspire to be like him. Ultimately, you will not be disappointed. He will most certainly reward your faith.

James Long

Week 1

New Beginnings

BRAND NEW START

Christians have an edge in the New Beginnings Department. God is stirring inside us, prompting change, urging us toward newness. Now, how do those changes happen?

Weekend Reading

I used to have a sign collection. No big deal, I guess. Except that I collected signs *wherever I found them.* Interesting decor: Early American Road Sign. Against one wall leaned a large, yellow, diamond-shaped sign, warning of a sharp left ahead. Next to it stood a fluorescent orange cone—the kind they use to mark construction zones. Two other signs, "borrowed" from a gas station (if I remember correctly) and from a funeral home, had been attached together to proclaim "SERVE YOURSELF FUNERALS." I was particularly proud of one sign, half the width of my room, with foot-high letters and an arrow; it said, "BUNNIES!" Someone who was selling the furry critters now had a sign to replace. On a shelf next to it, stood a flashing yellow caution light, extracted (with some difficulty) from a roadside sawhorse.

Interestingly, all of these "collectibles" disappeared from my room one warm July morning, the summer of My Big Change. I threw them all away.

I used to cuss constantly. I felt sophisticated. Or cool. Or something. That also disappeared the summer of My Big Change.

More significantly, I used to be bitter. Someone quite close to me had wronged me, and it hurt deeply. I thought I could never forgive him. In fact, I had no desire to forgive him, he so deserved my bitterness. I was astounded when I found those feelings leaving me the summer of My Big Change.

If I gave it some more thought, I'm sure I could add six or eight other changes that came to me that summer. Changes I never would have anticipated and, in several cases, did not notice at the time. Although it is true that all this redirection fell on me abruptly that one summer, these changes had been at work deep inside me for some time; they simply rose to the surface all at once. Gradually, unnoticed even by me, I had been *becoming difficult* for some time. Then one day—or more accurately, one summer—I *became different*, for all to see.

My friends noticed and were bewildered but couldn't quite put it into words. My brother could, and he mentioned the change at home: "Mom, what's happened to Jim?" My pastor commented (also to my mom): "I would have believed it about anybody but Jim."

This made me sound like a hardened criminal (my mother, ever loyal, was offended). Actually, others reacted so strongly not because I was so wicked but because the change was so sudden and so complete. I had become new. I thought differently, so I acted differently. At some level, life started over again.

Christians are committed to the idea that people can change.

I don't have to be the same this year as I was last year. Nor do you. We can improve. We can become new. Life can start all over again. We can startle our family and friends with a good new beginning.

> *"If anyone is in Christ, he is a new creation; the old has gone, the new has come!" (2 Corinthians 5:17).*

Unfortunately, Christians often display quite the opposite. You wonder where "the new" is; "the old" is so
commanding. So apparent. We say, "Good news! Jesus
makes us better," but our morals may be ugly as sin.

Or, perhaps you've noticed, there might be a dramatic
change, followed sometime later by a discouraging
regression. Christians fall, and sometimes the fall is
quite hard. "Jesus in me": now you see him, now
you don't.

And then we must also admit: people who aren't
Christian at all may experience dramatic change for
the better. Non-Christians improve too. Sometimes
people who make no claim to our label—CHRISTIAN—
are far more pleasant to be around. More kind. More
honest. More forgiving.

Even so, Christians have an edge in the New Beginnings Department. God is stirring inside us, prompting
change, urging us toward newness.

> *"He who began a good work in you will carry it on to
> completion until the day of Christ Jesus. . . . There-
> fore, my dear friends, . . . continue to work out your
> salvation with fear and trembling, for it is God who
> works in you to will and to act according to his good
> purpose" (Philippians 1:6; 2:12–13).*

When a person becomes a Christian—trusting Jesus,
confident that his death and resurrection make forgiveness possible—a process is set in motion. God
keeps working on us to cause our character to match
the character of Jesus himself. It doesn't happen all at
once. We may not necessarily feel new. Others may see

the changes before we do. But the goodness that comes from God is bubbling under the surface; later, or perhaps sooner, it will erupt, rising to express itself outwardly.

When the Big Change comes, what will it look like?

In what sense are *changed* Christians different?

Some people insist that they will actually, physically, look different. Neater. More modest. More *mature.*

Some sort of surface change may happen. But anyone can put on a clean shirt. The real changes are deeper. And far more important. A shift takes place in the character. We react to problems differently. A calmness settles over us that we can't quite account for apart from God's good work in us. We become nicer to be around. We are less defensive. Less jaded, cynical, sarcastic. We can put up with a lot without losing our patience. We find the capacity to forgive when wronged. We can stand up to our bad habits and resist the unhealthy influence of friends who believe differently than we do. Cleaner thoughts begin to fill our minds.

When the change really takes hold, people who know us begin to understand what it must have been like to have Jesus as a friend. We have become more like him than we ever would have dreamed.

Maybe we'll change our hobbies—the kinds of things we collect.

Our talk will no doubt improve.

We'll hold fewer grudges.

And our friends looking on may dare to think there's hope for them too.

"The fruit of the Spirit is love, joy, peace, patience, kindness, goodness, faithfulness, gentleness and self-control" (Galatians 5:22–23).

✓ Monday Checkpoint:
New Beginnings

Here's the truly astounding thing: People can change. We've all met people we would like to see changed. Some people are consistently obnoxious. Others are fine most of the time, till their annoying bad habits recur. We all see people we would like to make improvements on. Sometimes we find that person when we look in the mirror.

☞ Think about it . . .

Christianity makes an outrageously encouraging claim: God will change you. Christ will improve you. The Spirit will remake you. This is great news. Who is satisfied to stay the same?

Some people have given up hope that they can be better. Others shun the hard work they figure it would take to improve. Maybe these people would say, "Oh, I'm fine just the way I am."

Are you?

What if you really could be more loving—a better friend to people? What if there was a way to unlock the secret of joy, even when circumstances were kind of crummy? What if you could be more peaceful when life around you was spinning in turmoil?

Sure you'd be interested. And the amazing thing is, this is the hope God holds out to you. Take hold of it, and hang on!

☞ God's Word says . . .

"If anyone is in Christ, he is a new creation; the old has gone, the new has come!" (2 Corinthians 5:17).

☞ Make it a prayer . . .

Today, Lord, fill me with hope that I can be a brand new "me."

New Beginnings

Christians say a person changes completely when he or she opens up to God. If that's true, how does it happen? And why are some Christians still so unpleasant? So unkind? So unchanged?

☞ Think about it . . .

What happens deep inside to spark change is mysterious. Somehow, when true faith happens, a process starts. Like planting a seed. What do you do with the seed? You stick it in the ground, and for some time all you see is dirt. It doesn't look too promising. Where's the new life that's supposed to spring up?

Well, if that seed gets the water, nutrients, and sunlight it requires, it will begin to grow. Eventually, a shoot will poke through the dirt, reaching for the sun. If you're not looking quite carefully, you might never notice it. You'd be convinced there was still nothing there but dirt.

What do others see when they look at you? What do you see when you look at yourself? Are you encouraged by the growth in your life? Or are you still staring at a heap of dirt? Don't be discouraged. If your faith is true, the seed has been planted. New life has begun. The change will soon appear for all to see.

☞ God's Word says . . .

"He who began a good work in you will carry it on to completion until the day of Christ Jesus" (Philippians 1:6).

☞ Make it a prayer . . .

Lord, encourage me today. Help me see the growth that you are bringing about in me.

New Beginnings

Christians have an edge in the New Beginnings Department. God *is* stirring inside us, prompting change, urging us toward newness. Of course, sometimes people who make no claim to the label "CHRISTIAN" are far more pleasant to be around. More kind. More honest. More forgiving. What gives?

☞ Think about it ...

I remember talking to someone once who was not a Christian. I was trying to persuade him that he needed Jesus. When I talked about the kinds of changes Christ could bring to his life, he said he was satisfied with his life. When I told him he was a sinner, as we all are, he told me he felt like he was better than most people. When I told him he could be better, he told me Christians had disappointed him.

I have known people who did not claim to be Christian but who were simply better people than most Christians I knew. More gracious. More generous. More self-sacrificing. More loving.

I don't follow Christianity because it works. I follow it because I believe it to be true. But I do want to see faith at work also. Christians ought to be the most gracious, generous, self-sacrificing, loving people on the planet. So, I'll look at me, you look at you, then let's ask ourselves the question: How are we doing? How's the change coming?

☞ God's Word says ...

"Do not conform any longer to the pattern of this world, but be transformed by the renewing of your mind" (Romans 12:2).

☞ Make it a prayer ...

Lord, today I offer myself to you. I want to be your living sacrifice.

✔ Thursday Checkpoint:
New Beginnings

Let's say you have a job to do. It is a hard job. Very demanding. Sometimes you feel confident, but often you feel weak. And always, always you face this task that must be done. At times you feel discouraged, the demands are so great, the obstacles insurmountable. But suppose you could be teamed up with someone infinitely stronger and wiser. Someone who would willingly shoulder the load. Wouldn't that change everything?

☞ Think about it . . .

Anyone who takes faith seriously feels discouraged at times. We know what it is to try to improve yet fall short.

Of course, some Christians do not take faith seriously. They want to be part of the family, but they don't particularly want to act like the Father.

The Bible has an important message for all of us, whether we are taking faith seriously or just drifting along. God expects us to work at our faith—after all, *he is*. Christ is actively involved, the stronger and wiser big brother, helping us carry the load.

☞ God's Word says . . .

"Continue to work out your salvation with fear and trembling, for it is God who works in you to will and to act according to his good purpose" (Philippians 2:12–13).

☞ Make it a prayer . . .

Thank you for coming alongside me to enable me to do what I could never do on my own. Today, Lord, motivate me to work at my faith, side by side with you.

New Beginnings

When the change comes, what will it look like? If God is doing something in you, how will you know? If you are improved by God, what will get better?

☞ Think about it . . .

Take a snapshot of yourself before and after Jesus. What's the difference?

Try this. Divide a piece of paper into three sections. In one section, write: "Since becoming a Christian, I am more . . ." In the second section, write: "Since becoming a Christian, I am less . . ." Take a few minutes to write down some ideas.

As you did this, what kinds of things popped into your mind? What does the change look like? How are you different? How do you *want* to be different?

In the third section of your paper, write: "Since becoming a Christian, I want to be . . ."

You want to be what? More loving? Less angry? More kind? Less impatient? More "clean"? Less manipulative? How has becoming a Christian changed your goals for yourself?

You see, at the heart of what God is doing in you, is this one big change: He is giving you new desires. He is changing what you *want* to be. In this book, we will explore nine qualities that will change your life. They all begin here. With a desire to be new.

☞ God's Word says . . .

"The fruit of the Spirit is love, joy, peace, patience, kindness, goodness, faithfulness, gentleness and self-control" (Galatians 5:22–23).

☞ Make it a prayer . . .

Thank you, Lord, for giving me new desires. Change me! Change me! Change me!

Week 2

The Fruit of the Spirit Is Love

DEEP LOVE, COSTLY CHOICE

People sense something of what God must be like when we choose to care for them, help them, be kind to them, without expectation of return.

Weekend Reading

When I met Jan, I began to understand love. It's not that I had never been on the giving or receiving end of affection before. I never had reason to question my mom's loyalty and care, for instance. And though I fought with my brother, we were close. I felt protective of my sister, and I knew my dad, in his way, was committed to me. I had a girlfriend at the time, and we had a mutual thing going that we labeled "love"; and on some level, I suppose, that is what it was. But it wasn't like *this* love.

Jan was different.

What reason did she have to care for me?

I could say, for example, that my mom *had* to love me. It went with her job description as "mom." Same with my father and siblings. Family loyalty ought to count for something. As for my girlfriend: One, our relationship was reciprocal—we each gave with some expectation of return; and, two, it was clouded with infatuation. Was that really love at the core?

But Jan *was* different.

She opened my mind to a new way of seeing love for what it is supposed to be. Why? Because for Jan love was a costly choice.

For Jan love was a costly choice because she was sick. Her kidney disease acquainted her with pain, and pain can be a powerful distraction. Pain screams at you to focus inwardly, on yourself. Jan fought through that cloud of discomfort to reach toward me, and others, with love and concern. She was one of those people in whom you just naturally confided. She was easy to talk to because she was a good listener who obviously cared and always had something positive and encouraging to say. And she could "read" you—she seemed to sense when you were down or were feeling crummy, even before a word was spoken. If you had so much as a headache, much less a heartache, Jan seemed to know it, and even though she was in far greater discomfort, she could find the way to express her care. In the process, she gave love definition for me.

Love is not selfish.

For Jan, love was a costly choice because, in some ways at least, I was not particularly lovable at the time. Jan and her fiancé worked with students at our small Southern California church. Most of us were disinterested, rowdy, moderately rebellious. I was. But Jan did not withhold her concern until I settled down and got religious. Nor was she judgmental . . . just kind. Relentlessly so. And she showed me how love acts.

Love takes the first caring step.

And it does not stop.

I will never forget Jan's funeral. Her disease had won. But looking back now, I see something clearly I could not have anticipated then. When she was buried at Rose Hills Memorial Park, I thought that something inside me would die and be buried along with her. Instead, something inside me was born, or set free. Today, in some measure, I express love as I saw it expressed through her. I cannot shake her influence. I open my

New Testament and read words about love that make
sense to me, because I saw them lived out in her life.

The invisible God becomes visible when we love.

*"Dear friends, let us love one another, for love comes
from God. Everyone who loves has been born of God
and knows God. Whoever does not love does not know
God, because God is love. This is how God showed his
love among us: He sent his one and only son into the
world that we might live through him. This is love:
not that we loved God, but that he loved us and sent
his Son as an atoning sacrifice for our sins. Dear
friends, since God so loved us, we also ought to love
one another. No one has ever seen God; but if we love
one another, God lives in us and his love is made
complete in us"* (1 John 4:7–12).

No one has ever seen God.

But if we love each other, God lives in us.

Our costly choice to love brings God out in the open.
People sense something of what God must be like
when they meet people who choose to care for them,
help them, be kind to them, without expectations of
return, nothing to be gained.

This is how God showed his love among us.

He sent his one and only Son.

This is how we show *God* to others:

We love.

Unselfishly.

Our confidence in God is sparked by love.

"We know that we live in him and he in us, because he has given us of his Spirit. And we have seen and testify that the Father has sent his Son to be the Savior of the world. If anyone acknowledges that Jesus is the Son of God, God lives in him and he in God. And so we know and rely on the love God has for us" *(1 John 4:13–16).*

We know that we live in God.

And that he lives in us.

We know and rely on the love God has for us.

God's selfless, giving love sparks our confidence in him into a flame of trust.

We know that God has our best interests at heart. Trust comes much easier when we begin to see that we are the object of his love.

This same thing happens in all of our relationships. Conflicts in the family or with friends melt away under the heat of trusting, dependable love. Such love overcomes our jealousies, makes us want to act responsibly, prompts us to do what's right and good.

Real love, the best love, is reliable.

Fear is obliterated by love.

"God is love. Whoever lives in love lives in God, and God in him. In this way, love is made complete among us so that we will have confidence on the day of judgment, because in this world we are like him.

There is no fear in love. But perfect love drives out
fear, because fear has to do with punishment. The
one who fears is not made perfect in love" (1 John
4:16–18).

It really is difficult to separate love—the real and best
and reliable love—from God. Such love is so much at
the center of his nature. But isn't it astounding to discover that our experience of such love can so completely change us?

We try to reform ourselves through rules and regulations and promises that we will change. We will follow
a new pattern of life. We will break bad habits; we are
determined to do so.

Efforts at self-improvement can be so weak.

But this perfect love from God, alive within us through
faith in him, begins to bring the changes that our good
intentions could not deliver. In the process, our fears
begin to fall away. The barrier between us and God
crumbles. Guilt diminishes.

Something takes the panic out of knowing that God
always sees us.

Something gives us confidence.

That something is love.

When we live in it.

And it lives in us.

Because *in this world* we are like him.

If we are like God, even in this world, characterized by a
constantly deepening, unselfish love, what is there to fear?

We are being made perfect.

In love.

There is a way to prove our love for God, and it is our love for others.

> *"We love because he first loved us. If anyone says, 'I love God,' yet hates his brother, he is a liar. For anyone who does not love his brother, whom he has seen, cannot love God, whom he has not seen. And he has given us this command: Whoever loves God must also love his brother"* (1 John 4:19–21).

We don't like tests. And the more our grade hangs on a test, the less we like it.

Here's a test.

Pass/fail.

And the entire grade rests on the results.

Not a test to get into heaven exactly. But surely a test of whether faith is changing us. And the test is this: Do we love people? Even hard-to-like people?

It used to bother me and confuse me that the Bible said, "Anyone who does not love his brother whom he has seen, cannot love God, whom he has not seen."

I would protest: it is easier to love God, whom I've not seen. When I see someone, I see his weaknesses. That makes him harder to love. It is so difficult to love people because they are imperfect; because they offend me; because I can see them, and all about them that I dislike. So why should love of visible sinners be the gauge for my love for the invisible perfect God?

The reason, of course, is that in God's scheme of things, love is a costly choice. It is something that is expressed unconditionally, in spite of what I see, not because of what I see.

But I reserve my love for the lovely people. It's fun to love God. And I love my friends, particularly when they say nice things about me. I love my girlfriend, my girlfriend loves me.

Loving people who love me is not the test of love; that's just writing my name at the top of the paper. The test really starts with the question: "Can you love offensive people? Abusive people? Hard-to-love people? Can you love when it's costly? Can you love when pain or your own needs distract you?"

The point, hard as it might be to accept, is this: love for God and love for people—all people—are inseparable.

And that's what my friend Jan understood so well.

And that's why her love for me caused me to love not only her, but her God as well.

"The fruit of the Spirit is love"
(Galatians 5:22).

The Fruit of the Spirit Is Love

How does it feel when someone treats you like a friend? How does it feel when someone is kind to you without expecting anything in return? How does it feel to be loved? Picture the feeling. Then realize: this is a feeling you can give away.

☞ Think about it ...

Most of us grew up in a circle of love, from our earliest years—right from the beginning, in fact. Most of us had someone hovering over us, meeting our needs when we were too helpless to meet our own needs. Someone took care of us because of love. As the years passed, relatives and friends helped shape our definition of love, and they did that through their unselfish concern.

We know what love is like: unselfishly meeting someone's needs and doing so because you care. This is why it is so remarkable when we meet someone who is neither family nor friend yet loves us unselfishly. The Bible teaches us to treat even enemies with such love.

It is a high goal. When you see such love forming within, you will know for certain that God is alive in you.

☞ God's Word says ...

"Love your enemies.... If you love those who love you, what reward will you get?... Be perfect, therefore, as your heavenly Father is perfect" (Matthew 5:44, 46, 48).

☞ Make it a prayer ...

Lord, I have a hard enough time showing love to my family and friends, and here you expect me to love even my enemies! Okay, help me. Show me how. My life is yours.

The Fruit of the Spirit Is Love

God is invisible. But you can show people exactly what he looks like. All you have to do is love.

☞ Think about it . . .

When I first met Jan, whom I talked about at the beginning of this chapter, I was impressed with her. She was so different. I had probably met others who were unselfish, as she was, but I hadn't really noticed it. I had met nice people, but Jan was exceptionally nice.

As I got to know her better, I realized it was God who made her different. He was at work within her. I was no less impressed with her, of course, but now I was also taken with her God. I discovered something of what he looked like, because I could see love in Jan, my unselfish friend.

Who do you know who needs to see God?

You can be the one to reveal him. Your love will make him known.

☞ God's Word says . . .

"Dear friends, since God so loved us, we also ought to love one another. No one has ever seen God; but if we love one another, God lives in us and his love is made complete in us" (1 John 4:11–12).

☞ Make it a prayer . . .

Lord, give me practical, creative ideas. Teach me ways to show love, and in showing love, to show you to friends who need to see you.

The Fruit of the Spirit Is Love

If you know someone loves you, and that love will never change—it will never let you go—finally, you can relax. When you know you are held by an unselfish love, you just feel at home. You can be yourself.

☞ Think about it ...

I can talk about my friend Jan, and how remarkably kind she was. I can tell you how she redefined love for me. But what she really did, was to point me to a greater love—the love of God. As I felt at home in the love of God, my life changed, as hers had. I became new. God moved into my life, and I was glad to make room for him. Because of his love, I knew God had my best interests at heart. It was easy to trust him, because I knew I was the object of his love.

Now, in my friendships and in the way I treat my family, I want to copy that reliable love of his. I want my friends to know they can count on me. I want the members of my family to know they are appreciated. I want my love to earn their trust.

When I encounter misunderstanding, when I feel impatient, when I am misunderstood, when I am tempted to act selfishly, how will reliable love act?

☞ God's Word says ...

"We know and rely on the love God has for us" (1 John 4:16).

☞ Make it a prayer ...

Among my friends and with my family today, help me to display a trustworthy love.

The Fruit of the Spirit Is Love

I know God loves me, and that I love God, because I am not afraid of him anymore. I know he only wants to love me.

☞ Think about it . . .

"God is love." 1 John 4:16 says that. Think about those three words and the world of meaning they contain. Say it out loud: "God is love." Now say it like this: "GOD is love." What does it mean to you that God himself is described this way? Say it like this: "God IS love." Amazing, the certainty of it. Now say it this way: "God is LOVE." Of all the words he could have chosen to describe himself, he selected this one.

Now here's the astounding thing: about thirty words later, it says: "In this world we are like him" (1 John 4:17). Let that sink in. In this world, you can be like God, sharing something of his character, reminding others of him.

If God is love and we are like him, why would we ever be afraid of him again?

☞ God's Word says . . .

"There is no fear in love. But perfect love drives out fear, because fear has to do with punishment. The one who fears is not made perfect in love" (1 John 4:18).

☞ Make it a prayer . . .

In this world, Lord, I want to be like you. When people see me, I want them to be reminded of the God who loves them. Thank you for taking my fear away, and replacing it with trust.

✓ Friday Checkpoint:

The Fruit of the Spirit Is Love

I fell in love. I wanted to tell the girl, but at first the words felt awkward. They didn't feel awkward for long, however. The more I loved, the more I wanted to tell her. The more I *had* to tell her.

☞ Think about it . . .

We love God, because God first loved us. Of course, this is quite different from any other love we have felt. We can't see God. We can't hear his voice. We talk to him, but there is no audible response.

On the other hand, when we read Scripture or think about all God has done for us, he may seem quite close, even though he is unseen. At times, we may feel as if he has spoken with us, although his voice is unheard. We may feel loved by him, even though we have never felt his touch.

So how do you say "I love you" to an invisible, inaudible friend? How do you show God that you care? He says that we show our love for him by loving people. Think of someone in your life who needs your concern. Your care for that person is your love note to God.

☞ God's Word says . . .

"[God] has given us this command: Whoever loves God must also love his brother" (1 John 4:21).

☞ Make it a prayer . . .

Today, Lord, show me three practical ways I can express concern for people. Accept this care I show to people as my love note to you.

Week 3

The Fruit of the Spirit Is Joy

REASON FOR JOY

Happiness may come naturally when circumstances are naturally nice. But when things go wrong, bringing disappointment or sadness, where can we turn to find joy and hope?

Weekend Reading

As night fell, quiet filled up the valleys and settled over the hills. In the fields, talk died down to a whisper and then silenced altogether. Without city lights to dim the view, stars blazed through the blackness overhead like the suns that they are. Vivid. Close. The campfire, which hours before crackled and sparked, now hissed and smoldered, glowing only faintly. And shepherds dozed.

It was quite a birth announcement that stirred those herdsmen from slumber. Angels lit up the night sky and filled the countryside with their good news: a special baby had entered the world. The King had left the magnificence of his kingdom. The Creator had left the warmth of the womb.

There was good news.

And there was great joy.

Later. Another time and place. The news was not good, and yet there, too, this unquenchable joy prevailed.

The conditions could scarcely have been worse. It was cold, dark, damp, musty, rat-infested, unsanitary. Two men sat, their arms shackled in heavy iron chains, their feet secured in stocks; they could not turn or shift to a more comfortable position on the hard stone floor. Their backs had been beaten raw by civil authorities earlier in the day. Now their dirt-crusted, oozing wounds rubbed against rough stone walls. Yet in the absolute darkness of this inner cell, those two men,

Paul and his friend Silas, cruelly treated and wrongly incarcerated, decided to sing.

There was bad news.

Yet there was deep joy.

How could this be?

Joy flows out of upbeat experiences, logically, expectedly. We ace the test. We get the part. We win the scholarship. We are offered the job.

She says, "Yes."

Things go well for us and positive emotions bubble. But what is truly perplexing is when things turn sour for someone and he or she finds, somehow, a sustaining joy. A hope.

The response is unnatural. Yet I have seen it. Have you?

The test failed. The part goes to someone else. The scholarship is withheld. The job falls through.

She says, "Get lost!"

Or worse.

I have seen families fall apart or someone face major sickness or a friend's death, and out of the pain and confusion, hope comes to life. And, sometimes, an odd joy.

I do not mean weirdness. Or understandable denial.

But a sort of confidence and, well, joy that is not tied to the downswing or upturn of circumstance. If you've ever encountered someone with this quality, it pumps you with hope.

And curiosity.

How can they face bad news with good joy? What force pours hope into these people when they have every good reason to feel hopeless?

I stood at the bedside of a sick friend, a month or so before she died. It was Christmas time and the family and a few friends had gathered at her bedside to sing carols. At their request, I had brought my guitar and wound up leading the singing. As I played, I looked down at her in the subdued shadows of the holiday candles and twinkling lights. For those few moments at least, calmness and joy overcame pain.

What was it? Gratitude for family? Pleasant memories of the season? Yes. But for her it was also the truth in those songs we sang, those songs she moved her lips to because she couldn't sing.

Joy to the world, the Lord has come.

Now we need not fear the grave, Jesus Christ has come to save. Christ was born for this!

Joy is a choice.

And it is possible in most any circumstance.

Now this sounds truly weird, if when I say "joy" you hear "happiness." But joy and happiness are not equals. At least not the way Christians understand the words. Christians claim that crummy circumstances need not dictate my frame of mind. I can rise above the worst of life's experiences. There is a resource that injects hope into the most hopeless situations. And at some level, plugging into this source of hope and joy is a choice.

"Rejoice in the Lord always. I will say it again: Rejoice!... Do not be anxious about anything" (Philippians 4:4,6).

I find joy in spite of circumstance, because I know I'm loved.

I don't "rejoice" in failing the test or losing the part, the scholarship, the job or the girl. I rejoice, as the Bible puts it, "in the Lord." And I can push past anxiety through prayer, and through focusing my thinking on better things than my mishaps and disheartening experiences (Philippians 4:6–9).

Now all this has a sugar-sweet religious ring to it.

Words with their own shimmering halos.

I have concluded, however, that it is more than nice, hopeful talk.

I spoke with a girl once who had been blindsided by her parents' divorce. She had spent a few weeks with a relative, but when it was time to come home, her mom urged her to stay a bit longer. A few weeks later, when her mom picked her up at the airport, it was to drive her to the apartment that was to be their new home. They sat together in the car, at the curb, at "home," and she learned for the first time the extent of her parents' struggles.

She was understandably devastated. That did not surprise me. What did surprise me was the hope that held
her together. And the joy that settled into her. And the
conviction that far above the circumstances that
brought her pain and rejection she could hold on to the
close hand of a loving God.

Far above. And close.

Pain. And joy.

She was a new Christian, and this was the first great
test of her faith. She told me how she had cried that
night in loneliness and bewilderment, but also how
she began to sense the Lord—his closeness and his
care. Her new Christian friends expressed concern,
and in that concern, she felt the arms of God. She still
felt pain and confusion at times, but even in the midst
of those difficult times, there was also a feeling that
could only be described as "joy."

"I will say it again: Rejoice!"

Joy is most clearly revealed not in good times, but in bad.

When circumstances are good, joy may be little more
than happiness. Which is okay as far as it goes. But joy
goes much further. When circumstances are bad, yet
we find joy and hope, there is a strong and deep quality to such joy.

*"Consider it pure joy, my brothers, whenever you face
trials of many kinds, because you know that the testing
of your faith develops perseverance" (James 1:2–3).*

We would not naturally put "joy" and "trials," "faith" and "perseverance" in the same sentence. But life as we must live it often pushes them toward one another. If I am to live joy and faith, I must learn to do so with trials and in perseverance. In fact, life as it faces me, with its trials, can feed my joy as it feeds my faith. Hardship strengthens my faith. And such strength brings joy.

This unexpected joy flows out of a new perspective.

A different way of looking at life. Whether the times are good or bad.

Joy is possible—and hope too—because we can catch a view of God's *long-term purpose*, even though there may be little or no *short-term relief*. Think again of my dying friend, confined to that hospital bed in the family room of her home. There was no short-term relief for her, but she did catch a glimpse of God's long-term purpose. Soon, her pain would fade and cease; she would be released from cancer's grip; she would finally see Jesus, and this filled her with hope.

In other words, joy sees beyond today. Way beyond. Joy is content to have a positive fix on the overall outcome of life—and beyond life—without necessarily having the specifics of God's agenda (and timetable) nailed down.

Sounds philosophical. But "philosophy" can be helpful. It helped my other friend in the wake of her parents' unexpected divorce.

The point can be distilled to profound simplicity: God loves me. God is in charge. Even if hateful things happen. Even if God waits to change what is bad.

The Bible talks a lot about hope and joy, almost interchangeably, and ties them both to the future. A view of the future that invades the troubles of today, leaving traces of this hope and joy.

> *"You greatly rejoice, though now for a little while you may have had to suffer grief in all kinds of trials. These have come so that your faith—of greater worth than gold, which perishes even though refined by fire—may be proved genuine and may result in praise, glory and honor when Jesus Christ is revealed. Though you have not seen him, you love him; and even though you do not see him now, you believe in him and are filled with an inexpressible and glorious joy, for you are receiving the goal of your faith, the salvation of your souls" (1 Peter 1:6–9).*

The Bible is filled with these thoughts. Repeated throughout its pages is the idea that you can face most anything without coming unglued because of a hope in the future that brings a deep joy into today. The early Christians needed to hear this talk, because they were faced with circumstances that often turned toward pain.

Our circumstances may often turn toward happiness, and only occasionally toward pain, but when life gets perplexing, there is a limitless resource.

Even when faced with bad news there can be deep joy.

The man struggles to remain conscious. He has been beaten to the point of disfigurement, hardly recognizable, even by his friends. He stands, dizzy, in the center of swirling confusion. His eyes strain to focus, to pull order out of the blur of faces surrounding him. Angry, jeering voices rise in a thunderous commotion. A dark figure grabs him, spins him, slaps him, strips him. Naked and bleeding, he is pushed off balance to the rocky ground, then pulled sideways and onto rough, splintery timbers, his arms stretched wide and held. A spike is positioned at the wrist, a hammer raised . . .

> *"Let us fix our eyes on Jesus, the author and perfecter of our faith, who for the joy set before him endured the cross, scorning its shame, and sat down at the right hand of the throne of God. Consider him who endured such opposition from sinful men, so that you will not grow weary and lose heart" (Hebrews 12:2–3).*

Consider him. Who, for the joy of perfecting our faith, endured. Who opened the way for hope.

And joy.

Regardless of our circumstances.

"The fruit of the Spirit is . . . joy"
(Galatians 5:22).

The Fruit of the Spirit Is Joy

Good stuff happens; we feel great. Life turns crummy; we feel down. But there is a sort of joy that is not tied to the downswing or upturn of circumstance. We can find encouragement, even when life itself is most discouraging.

☞ Think about it . . .

When angels appeared to shepherds that first Christmas evening, the air itself was charged with life! How could those herdsmen help but feel happy? Years later, Paul and his friend found themselves locked up in a prison that smelled of death itself. How could they help but feel depressed?

Okay, so why were they singing?

If you don't get the job; if you fail the test; if you aren't chosen for the scholarship; if you watch a friendship fall apart; even then, can you find a place of joy, deep inside you? If the news is worse yet, is joy possible? Only if your confidence and hope is rooted in a close relationship with God. If he is close, the trouble and turmoil can be quite deep, without sweeping us away. We may still *feel* down—that is understandable. But stirring somewhere within us, there can be a spark of hope, a flicker of joy, because we know the love of God.

☞ God's Word says . . .

"Rejoice in the Lord always. I will say it again: Rejoice! . . . Do not be anxious about anything" (Philippians 4:4, 6).

☞ Make it a prayer . . .

Today, Lord, regardless of what comes my way, let me feel your nearness and experience your joy.

✓ Tuesday Checkpoint:

The Fruit of the Spirit Is Joy

The teenage girl was blind-sided by her parents' divorce. She knew there were problems but had no idea they were this serious. When she was surprised with the bad news, did God expect her to jump up and down, praising the Lord?

☞ Think about it . . .

We say that people can find reason for hope—even joy—in the midst of the worst of life's experiences. That doesn't mean life does not sometimes hurt. It doesn't mean God expects us to deny pain and disappointment.

The Bible says, "Rejoice in the Lord always." It would be impossible to "rejoice always" if it weren't for those three key words, "in the Lord." We don't get all thrilled and happy because we're having hardship; that kind of denial is silly. Our encouragement, our hope, our joy is *in the Lord*. A caring God is close. We hold on to him.

Instead of denying our problems, he invites us to bring them to him (Philippians 4:6). We place our worries in his open hands and find his peace, hope, even joy.

What concerns are you carrying today that need to be handed over to the God who loves you?

☞ God's Word says . . .

"I will say it again: Rejoice! . . . The peace of God, which transcends all understanding, will guard your hearts and your minds in Christ Jesus" (Philippians 4:4, 7).

☞ Make it a prayer . . .

Lord, with your help, I want to exchange my worries for your joy. Thanks for your loving concern.

The Fruit of the Spirit Is Joy

All kinds of things can cause joy. Good times and happy circumstances naturally put smiles on our faces. But is it possible to find reason for joy even in the tough times?

☞ Think about it . . .

Each day is crammed with good gifts from God, excellent reasons for joy. The gift of friendship. The gift of laughter. Parents who care for us. The beauty of a perfect day. Music and art. Ideas and conversation. Health. Life itself. God gives his gifts and we receive them with joy. We en*joy* them.

Our days are also filled with good gifts we might not naturally call good. Pain can be good for us if it alerts us to a problem we must correct. Criticism can cause us to see something that must be changed. Failure can point the way to greater growth. If we can find purpose in them, even negative things can seem positive.

God uses every circumstance, no matter how painful, to strengthen us. We are better people because of what we endure. God does not waste anything, even hardship. Because of this, we can consider it joy, even when tough times come.

☞ God's Word says . . .

"Consider it pure joy, my brothers, whenever you face trials of many kinds, because you know that the testing of your faith develops perseverance" (James 1:2–3).

☞ Make it a prayer . . .

Today, Lord, as I face those things that try my patience and test my faith, remind me that you are alive in me. Nothing I endure is wasted.

✓ Thursday Checkpoint:

The Fruit of the Spirit Is Joy

If we want to unlock the secret of joy, we must find a new perspective. A new way of looking at life.

☞ Think about it ...

You open the box and empty its contents on the table. There, before you, are hundreds of individual pieces that, when fitted together, will create something that makes sense. A complete picture. You pick up individual pieces, look at them from different angles, and try your best to fit them together with other pieces. Slowly, the project takes shape, as you compare the puzzle on the table with the picture on the box—your only guide to what this puzzle is to become.

Your life is such a project. In time, hundreds, *thousands* of individual details will somehow fit together. When the puzzle is at last complete, you will be satisfied with the result. Until then, the process of figuring out each piece can be annoying, a seemingly endless trial of your patience.

The encouraging difference between these two puzzles is this: The puzzle that is your life, *God* is putting together. Each individual piece—whether hardship or happiness—God will fit together with flawless skill. When the process is complete, your life will perfectly match the picture in his mind—the perfect image of what you can become.

☞ God's Word says ...

"You greatly rejoice, though now for a little while you may have had to suffer grief in all kinds of trials" (1 Peter 1:6).

☞ Make it a prayer ...

Thank you, Lord, for giving us the big picture. Life will fit your purpose. You will give us joy.

The Fruit of the Spirit Is Joy

Have you ever stopped to think, what makes Jesus happy? What puts a smile on his face and brings him joy?

☞ Think about it . . .

What makes Jesus happy? What unlocks his joy? Why, you do, of course. He looks at you—at what you can become—and he feels deep happiness. He sees what can become of your character, and he is satisfied. He holds your image in his mind and is pleased.

What he sees when he looks at you, is someone who has been forgiven. The image he holds is the image of your character, shaped to perfection by faith and grace and time. When Christ looks at you, he sees the reflection of the character of God, and he knows you will be so changed, because he died to make it happen.

In fact, Jesus found so much joy in seeing what you would become, it gave him the strength to face his painful death. He knew the crucifixion would not end in his shame and agony— shame and agony were just the doorway to his joy. Through shame and agony, he would make forgiveness possible and would bring millions of changed people into the city of God.

☞ God's Word says . . .

"Let us fix our eyes on Jesus, the author and perfecter of our faith, who for the joy set before him endured the cross" *(Hebrews 12:2).*

☞ Make it a prayer . . .

Lord, help me to find my joy in pointing my friends to Jesus, who stands waiting and smiling for joy.

The Fruit of the Spirit Is Peace

PEACE ON EARTH ... IN ME

Those Christmas-card greetings sound so hopeful and upbeat, bringing visions of harmony and good will circling the globe. Back in the real world, we wonder, is peace even possible?

Weekend Reading

"Peace on earth!" It was an audacious proclamation. If history was anything, it was the chronicle of unrest, bloodshed, war. Worldwide hostility. Human hate. How could any one person make any difference at all? Let alone one dependent newborn?

"Peace on earth!" It was an ironic announcement. Not many months would pass before the regional authorities would issue a decree, condemning to death all male babies under the age of two. The arrival of one guiltless, peace-bringing baby would soon result in death to Bethlehem's other innocent infants.

"Peace on earth!" It was a contradictory statement. Peace? Earth? Could two more conflicting words be coupled?

It is a fair question.

How can Christians claim that peace has come when life itself says so plainly that it hasn't?

Perhaps all these Christmas cards we've received and read, signed and sent, have misled us.

"Peace on earth!" they tell us, as stars shine high above the stable and as the crude wooden manger emits its own unearthly glow. But read the words more closely. Didn't Saint Luke report the proclamation with a slight twist not found on all those holiday greetings?

"Glory to God in the highest," Luke said, "and on earth peace to men on whom his favor rests" (Luke 2:14).

(Older Bibles express it: "Good will toward men.")

In any case, the angels gave their message then returned to heaven, leaving earth to unravel the mystery of this peace. Leaving earth to go on spinning through space and time in its unchanging unrest.

Except for those who find God's favor.

They find peace.

Even here.

On earth.

But is that all there is to this peace? Private. Individual. For the favored.

An unknown war ends in peace.

We might not label it "war," but the unsettled feeling of unrest we understand. Maybe we're in conflict with a former friend, and we don't even remember what started it; who fired the first shot. Or there's friction between us and our parents, our brother, a coworker. But we can't quite pin it down. Somehow, we've found the distance growing between us—a wedge driven down, a separation. Someone has something against us, but we've forgotten what it is. Or we've never cared enough to find out.

God had something against us, too—all of us. A legitimate complaint. Long before we gave it any thought,

God had a gripe. The wedge was driven. The distance had grown to a gap that could never be closed. Still we didn't quite focus on the conflict. Perhaps we had a vague sense that all was not right in the universe, but would we have ever taken the necessary steps to bring peace? Could we?

Then, Christmas came.

An infant was laid down as a gift, in the middle of the conflict, halfway between the warring parties.

"Peace on earth!"

Through faith we find favor, and the battle between us and God ends in a truce. An alliance is forged. Friendship where there had been conflict.

> *"Since we have been justified through faith, we have peace with God through our Lord Jesus Christ ...*
>
> *"God demonstrates his own love for us in this: While we were still sinners, Christ died for us ...*
>
> *"For if, when we were God's enemies, we were reconciled to him through the death of his Son, how much more, having been reconciled, shall we be saved through his life!" (Romans 5:1, 8, 10).*

But the question persists: Is that all there is to this peace? Private. Individual. For the favored.

Well, even if this were all, it would be much. After all, there can be no greater conflict than to be at war with God; therefore, there can be no greater peace than to see that hostility with God come to an end.

Yet, there is more.

The churning feeling of inner turmoil is stilled.

We know what it is to be at war with ourselves. With our feelings. With the circumstances around us that somehow manage to crowd *into* us.

Think about the last time you felt deep guilt.

Or remember the knot in your stomach as you waited to see if something would turn out the way you hoped it would? Or how you feared it would?

Can you still feel the nervousness you experienced before an important test? When you weren't sure whether you'd be labeled "SUCCESS" or "FAILURE"?

Can you *feel* the question: "Will the people at the new school like me?" Or, "Will I get the job?" Or, "Will Mom and Dad work out their problems?" Or, "Will there be enough money for college?" Or, "Will Grandma's sickness end in death?"

And yet, something has happened.

"Peace on earth!"

As certainly as we can *feel* worries, we can find inner calm.

> *"Do not be anxious about anything, but in everything, by prayer and petition, with thanksgiving, present your requests to God. And the peace of God, which transcends all understanding, will guard your hearts and your minds in Christ Jesus" (Philippians 4:6–7).*

Christians gave the sentiment even deeper meaning, as if to say, "In the middle of any circumstance, God can give peace, and that's what I want for you." And so, having opened the secrets of private, individual peace, these people felt on obligation to point others away from conflict and turmoil, and deeper into peace.

The walls that divide people have been broken down.

And with the falling of the walls comes the prospect of peace between people.

It's now possible.

We don't have to hide behind the silly barriers of class and clique and race. That is, in fact, terribly wrong. It is at odds with all God is trying to do in the world.

Why is it that throughout history people who have claimed to know God have been so exclusive, so obnoxious toward those who are different? Even to the extent of violent persecution in the name of faith?

Yet, when God wanted to start something new in the world—"Peace on earth!"—he did not keep it as something private and individual. He expressed his peace toward us, in part, by peacefully grouping us with one another.

We were separated from God ... *"But now in Christ Jesus you who once were far away have been brought near through the blood of Christ" (Ephesians 2:13).*

We were separated also from one another, but ... *"[Christ] himself is our peace, who has made the two one*

*and has destroyed the barrier, the dividing wall of hostility
... His purpose was to create in himself one new man out of
the two, thus making peace ... He came and preached peace
to you who were far away and peace to those who were near.
For through him we both have access to the Father by one
Spirit" (2:14, 15, 17–18).*

You could think of it this way: The wooden cross on
which Jesus was executed was constructed out of the
barrier that once divided us. When you're tempted to
rebuild those walls between yourself and others,
remember where the building materials come from.
Leave those timbers alone.

To claim private, individual peace with God, to enjoy
the inner calm that knowing God can bring, and then
to go on fighting with others is unthinkable. To say
you know God, then toy with bigotry and racism is
intolerable. To be Christian, then be hateful toward
someone, or make fun of someone, or exclude someone
is inconsistent.

On the contrary, to be Christian means to work at
resolving conflicts between people. Knowing God
teaches us to resist hatred, bigotry, racism, division.
Enjoying peace with God motivates us to point others
toward him and the calmness he brings.

> *"Blessed are the peacemakers," Jesus said, "for they
> will be called sons of God" (Matthew 5:9).*

And I wonder, is "PEACEMAKER" a label we care to wear?

Well, if peace has come to us, we have no choice.

Peace is on tomorrow's agenda. God has plans for this planet. We can fully expect peace to sweep over it. Not today, perhaps, but certainly. Until he steps into our history again, in that direct and visible way, we are his representatives, passing on the news that is truly good:

Peace is possible.

With God.

With myself.

With you.

"The fruit of the Spirit is ... peace"
(Galatians 5:22).

✓ Monday Checkpoint:

The Fruit of the Spirit Is Peace

Let's suppose the good news is really true: Jesus came to bring peace. Now, pick up today's newspaper or tune in tonight's news. How do you think the headlines make Jesus feel? How would those headlines be rewritten, if Jesus' promise came true right now?

☞ Think about it . . .

Jesus' closest friends were impressed by how he prayed. When they observed Jesus, they concluded that prayer could be conversation—a conversation that brings calmness. Worry and agitation can be stilled through prayer. It is not too surprising that they wanted to know his secret.

In response to their questions, he taught them what we've come to call "The Lord's Prayer" (Matthew 6:5–13). What was the point? God deserves your respect, but you can talk to him as your Father. He is eager to listen. He is concerned about your needs and will care for you; you don't have to get uptight. The prayer also urges us to look at life differently. We're not "home" yet. The world is filled with turmoil; God's will is our peace. So we pray, "Your kingdom come, your will be done on earth as it is in heaven" (6:10).

When Christ returns, peace will cover the earth. Until then, we can find a place of stillness and calm within. This peace comes to us through prayer.

☞ God's Word says . . .

"Glory to God in the highest, and on earth peace to men on whom his favor rests" (Luke 2:14).

☞ Make it a prayer . . .

Thank you for the peace I feel when I remember your loving concern for me.

The Fruit of the Spirit Is Peace

You know the feeling: You've had a disagreement with a friend, and there's now something between you. The friendship is disrupted. You can *feel* the distance. And it's not a comfortable feeling.

☞ Think about it . . .

Families sometimes experience this sort of distance, too. It feels weird, because the people who ought to be the closest, almost feel like enemies. Maybe you've faced this when you have clashed with a brother or sister. Maybe you feel at odds with your parents. Or maybe you've watched as your own parents have drifted apart.

We've all experienced this same sort of disagreement between us and God, some of us without even knowing it or fully understanding it. The one person who loves us most, the one person, above all others, with whom we should be close, can instead seem so distant. In fact, the Bible says that as a people, our own moral wrongness had driven such a wedge between us and God that we were actually his "enemies."

Then God did for us what we must all do for our friends and family members: He took the first, most important step to make peace. It was costly. But, in his mind, well worth the price.

☞ God's Word says . . .

"Since we have been justified through faith, we have peace with God through our Lord Jesus Christ" (Romans 5:1).

☞ Make it a prayer . . .

Thank you, Lord, for making peace with me. Help me to take the first step in making peace with others.

The Fruit of the Spirit Is Peace

What do you do when you feel there is a war raging inside you? When you feel your problems are so much out of your control? How do you calm the inner churning and make peace?

☞ Think about it ...

The guy who said, "Do not be anxious about anything," was a prisoner at the time. The man who said the peace of God would calm us, was the same guy who had been beaten, ridiculed, shipwrecked, starved, and disappointed by friends. So, what was his secret? What was the key that unlocked his peacefulness?

He was certain of God's loving concern.

When he was nervous, he prayed. When he was frightened, he talked to God. When failure seemed certain, he discussed it with his unseen Father. When he was out of money; when friends turned against him; when he was hungry and tired and cold; when he wasn't sure what to do next; when he feared for his life; he prayed.

And when he prayed, convinced of God's concern, his worries settled down and he felt surrounded by the peace of God.

☞ God's Word says ...

"Do not be anxious about anything, but in everything ... present your requests to God. And the peace of God, which transcends all understanding, will guard your hearts and your minds in Christ Jesus" (Philippians 4:6–7).

☞ Make it a prayer ...

Lord, you know all that troubles me today, the things that would steal my peace. I place myself and my concerns in your strong and loving hands.

The Fruit of the Spirit Is Peace

Friendship is amazing! And what is it? Two people, sharing common ground.

☞ Think about it . . .

What brings us together as friends? Shared interests. Something we hold in common that is greater than the things that would divide us. Maybe it's a hobby we share, or similar tastes in music, or a common interest in sports. Out of our similarity, friendship grows.

At the same time, one of the things that makes a friendship interesting is *difference*. Our friends are like us, but also unlike us, and the dissimilarities add dimension. A friend shows us new ways of thinking of things, introduces new hobbies, shares other styles of music, brings a different background. Out of our dissimilarities, friendship deepens.

Faith does something truly astounding: It puts us all on common ground. It opens the way to friendship with people quite different from us. It gives us something to share, far greater than anything that could divide us.

As Christianity spread throughout the world, different races came together; the old prejudice and hatred fell away. Rich people and poor people discovered they were not as different as they had thought; in the eyes of God they were the same. God made peace between people, and those who saw it were amazed.

☞ God's Word says . . .

"[Christ] himself is our peace, who has made the two one and has destroyed the barrier, the dividing wall of hostility" (Ephesians 2:14).

☞ Make it a prayer . . .

Lord, help me to extend my circle of friends, to dare include those who are different from me.

The Fruit of the Spirit Is Peace

Suppose you open your life to God. You give him control. Okay, what changes?

☞ Think about it ...

What changes when you open your life to God? Well, everything.

One cool fall evening some friends and I were walking up and down Hollywood Boulevard, in Hollywood, California, talking to people about God—people who seemed curious or interested. Out of the crowd of mostly high-school and college-aged faces, an elderly gentleman approached me. He knew what I was doing, and he was smiling. There, at about 10 P.M., under a street light, with confusion all around us, *he* told *me* about God.

"Let me tell you how to read the New Testament book of Acts," he said, his voice hushed, excitement lighting his face. "Read the book of Acts with a question behind every adventure you encounter. And the question is, 'Under whose influence am I?'"

He was convinced, remarkable things happened to people then, and to us now, when God is the influence, when he is given the control. In the midst of life's greatest challenges, you will find peace, quietness, confidence, when you take your cues from God himself.

Think back over this past week. How would it have unfolded differently, had God been given greater control over you?

☞ God's Word says ...

"The fruit of righteousness will be peace; the effect of righteousness will be quietness and confidence forever" (Isaiah 32:17).

☞ Make it a prayer ...

Influence me, Lord. Control me today. Give me the peace, quietness and confidence that flow from a righteous life.

The Fruit of the Spirit Is Patience

PATIENCE: THE UNOPENED GIFT

If it must come through difficulty, we would just as soon do without it. But have you tried that?

Weekend Reading

I find impatient people amusing (and must, therefore, sometimes laugh at myself). There's just something about unbridled impatience that is humorous. The face reddens. Breathing comes in snorts and sighs. Eyeballs rolls up into the head. Arms fold. Feet shuffle nervously. Complaints come irrationally.

All rather amusing.

Okay, so I'm at Tasty Freeze with a couple of friends. It's about 8 P.M., Friday, and we are sitting outside at this picnic table across from the counter, grabbing something to eat after a game. Cars are coming and going as usual when suddenly this Chevy bounces up the driveway and into the lot. The driver slips it into neutral and blows out a month's worth of built-up carbon. Heads turn. The burgers suddenly taste like Shell unleaded premium exhaust, and the Cokes are recarbonated with carbon monoxide. We are not impressed.

This guy is obviously (key word) *impatient*. Is it the traffic in the parking lot, or what? There is a small clearing between cars so the driver pops the clutch, tires squealing briefly in protest. The car disappears behind the building and quickly reemerges in the shadows, away from the lights, on the other side of the Tasty Freeze. This guy just got here, but already he's leaving. Impatiently. What he obviously does not know (but we do) is that there is no driveway on this dark side of the building, just a taller-than-normal curb. At the table, burgers lower, eyes widen, no one speaks ... soon enough. As traffic on the highway clears, the Chevy lunges forward and there is a sudden deafening sound of metal Chevy-frame grinding concrete curb, followed by a stream of obscenities spilling out the open window.

And our sympathy merges with our amusement.

Is impatience ever productive?

I've seen people at banks and stores shift from line to line, looking for the quickest out. Maxim: The fastest line is the one you're not in.

A friend of mine, impatient with his girlfriend, decided to get even. They had argued about *something,* some insignificant and soon-forgotten conflict. Hard as he argued, loud as he yelled, he didn't get his way. She didn't cave in. Her stubbornness mirrored his own. He'd fix her. In his irrational impatience, he drove down to his U.S. Army recruiter and enlisted. This would get her attention. She'd be sorry she ever argued with him. Just wait till the military took him hundreds, perhaps thousands, of miles away. Then she'd miss him. Then she'd wish he was still there, at her side. Then she'd wish she'd given him his way. Returning to his car in the lot, the consequences of his impatient snit began to dawn on him. He was so shaken he backed his car into the side of the recruitment office. Yes, there were damages. That was okay, though, he paid for the repairs, you might say, with his time.

I once saw someone, in his impatience, toss a stool across a room. It broke. That sort of outburst always happens quickly. What invariably—and embarrassingly—goes much more slowly is picking up the pieces.

It seemed to take forever for the guy at the Tasty Freeze to get the front end of his Chevy back up onto the curb and to back the car around the parking lot so that he could exit out the only driveway, the one he entered through, in absolute humiliation.

Unchecked impatience often leads to humiliation.

I have heard people joke that they don't have the patience to develop patience, an understandable sentiment.

But how can you live without it?

Patience is part of a process to turn us into better people.

What frustrates us into impatience, and the anger that often goes with it, is our lack of control. Patience, then—and staying clear of anger—rests in somehow surrendering our strong desire to have control. If we can trust that someone better and stronger *is* in control, we can begin to let go of the frustration over how events are turning out.

How then do we develop such patience? Oddly, through the very thing that frustrates us: difficulty.

> *"We ... rejoice in our sufferings, because we know that suffering produces perseverance; perseverance, character; and character, hope. And hope does not disappoint us, because God has poured out his love into our hearts" (Romans 5:3–5).*

Perseverance, or patience, is the ability to hold up under difficult circumstances—the sort of circumstances that come naturally with life on a planet at odds with God. And patience grows as hardship comes. Our wrestling with the bad stuff of life teaches us perseverance.

Patience in turn improves our character. We know this. Some of the people we all most admire are people who do not lose their patience. People who stay pleasant when life doesn't.

And, as the Scripture presents it, this growing patience is linked to hope. We become people of hope, not people overcome with hopelessness. This happens because we know that God has an agenda for better things. A timeline to erase life's wrongs.

Until then, we wait. We hope. We learn patience. Perhaps we suffer. As we do, though, it is with the sense that God's loving concern for us is being poured out within us. The Bible claims this to be true. And many of us have experienced it ourselves and observed it in others.

The Bible teaches us the idea of patience through extremes.

It may at first sound like God does not have a whole lot to say about what triggers impatience in most of us. Consistently Christianity teaches patience, not through the small annoyances but through what we would all call an extreme: seemingly endless suffering.

We are not told how to be patient enough to stand in a check-out line without sighing. We are not instructed in the skill of patience to follow an incompetent driver. We are not given lessons on how to avoid impatience in a crowded Tasty Freeze lot when the front end of your

Chevy cascades over the curb. When Christianity talks about patience, it does not focus on the flu or poor grades or the trial of no Friday-night date.

Of course, God cares about our flu, our grades, our loneliness. And as we learn patience, a wait in line or a slow-moving lane or a congested parking lot should rattle us a lot less. But the more astounding point is this: Christianity is strong enough to carry us through the absolute worst life can toss at us. Even if unimaginable hardship drags on unending.

It is no joke that the Bible says, "Be patient" (how long?) "until the Lord's coming" (James 5:7). That may be a while. Yet, "The Lord is full of compassion and mercy" (5:11). We can count on his understanding and concern even if we must stretch our patience out for a lifetime of suffering.

Patience over things today is tied to, and cannot be separated from, things "tomorrow."

I confess. The idea stopped me for a moment: Even God has to exercise patience. He doesn't like life being strewn with hardship any more than we do. In fact, he likes it a lot less. Like us, he is saddened by the suffering in the world. He is eager to do away with it. It is his aching desire to change all that is wrong with life.

But he waits. Patiently.

And there is good reason for the waiting.

"Do not forget this one thing, dear friends: With the Lord a day is like a thousand years, and a thousand

*years are like a day. The Lord is not slow in keeping
his promise, as some understand slowness. He is
patient with you, not wanting anyone to perish, but
everyone to come to repentance. But the day of the
Lord will come ..." (2 Peter 3:8–10).*

Things will change.

Suffering will stop.

All the promises will be kept.

Patience, even long-term patience, will be rewarded.

But this making right of all that is wrong will also
bring to a close the opportunity for people to change.
To turn to God. So for now, God waits. Patiently.

We could say, "Patience is no big deal for God. Time
flies for him. Why, even a thousand years are like a
day." But couldn't we also say that God understands
the difficulty of our waiting? He is hurting with us.
Each minute that we must exercise patience, he is
patiently waiting with us. Each day of our hardship is
like a thousand years to him.

And so we learn patience from the extreme: Even if we
had to suffer every day, unending, throughout life, our
faith could support us in patience. Why? Because a patient God pours his love into us, even as he patiently waits
with us for the better things that certainly will come.

"The fruit of the Spirit is ... patience"
(Galatians 5:22).

The Fruit of the Spirit Is Patience

Next time you feel really, *really* impatient, try to hold that pose—don't change the expression on your face. Find a mirror and take a look. Pretty funny, huh?

☞ Think about it . . .

If patience must come through difficulty, we might just as soon do without it. But have you tried that?

Every day brings some exasperation—some need, small or great, to exercise patience. Patience is just part of the equipment we need if are going to cope with life.

Think through the past few weeks. What has tried your patience? A teacher who didn't understand you? A "friend" who annoyed you? A brother or sister in an obnoxious mood? A parent's expectations that seemed unreasonable? A lost job? A disappointing grade? A broken-down car? A busted stereo? Idiots in traffic? Sickness?

Put a check mark next to the problems over which you have some control. There may be something you can do to improve the situation and simplify your life. For most of us, though, after we've done all in our power, there's still a great deal that would make us impatient that is simply out of our control. We just have to live with it.

Now what?

Read the following verse. Do you suppose God could actually give you the power to be patient?

☞ God's Word says . . .

"Being strengthened with all power according to his glorious might so that you may have great endurance and patience" (Colossians 1:11).

☞ Make it a prayer . . .

You know my need, Lord. Give me the power to be patient.

✔ **Tuesday Checkpoint:**

The Fruit of the Spirit Is Patience

It doesn't just happen magically or automatically—I was an impatient person yesterday, *BAM!* I'm a patient person today. Patience is a process. Something we must learn. Now for the good news ...

☞ Think about it ...

The truly good news is, we can learn patience. It is a life-skill we can acquire. And we will be glad we did. The reward of patience is character. We become better.

Think about the people you most admire. What do you like about them? No doubt, many different things. Now, is impatience one of those traits you really appreciate in people? Is there anyone you could look in the eye and honestly say, "What I really like about you is your impatience"? "Ooo! I just love it when you lose your temper!" Probably not. We admire people who do not become unpleasant, even when life gets tough.

So where does patience come from? Unfortunately, it comes through unpleasantness. Hardship produces patience. Tough times bring about perseverance. Then, as patience grows, we become noticeably better people. It can be a difficult process, of course. But in the midst of it, we are never forgotten. God is always there, pouring his love into us.

☞ God's Word says ...

"We rejoice in our sufferings, because we know that suffering produces perseverance; perseverance, character; character, hope. And hope does not disappoint us, because God has poured out his love into our hearts" (Romans 5:3–5).

☞ Make it a prayer ...

Thanks for staying with me Lord, even through the toughest of times.

✓ Wednesday Checkpoint:
The Fruit of the Spirit Is Patience

I'm pretty sure I can be patient, just so I don't have to be patient for very long.

☞ Think about it . . .

Isn't this the problem with patience: we have to keep waiting just a little too long? You're running late, and you're stuck in the *slow* line. You can be patient, just so you don't have to be patient for long. Of all the drivers on earth, of all the highways on the planet, somehow you wind up behind the world's least competent driver. Okay, patience is possible, but for how long? You've become sick and you feel crummy. Your head aches, your stomach's churning, you feel exhausted. But you can handle it, just so you're feeling better by . . . oh, let's say, by noon?

Patience is no big deal, just so we can be quick about it.

The Bible does not tell us how to cope with long lines, incompetent drivers, or the flu. It does not promise quick relief when we are misunderstood or the demands on us are unrealistic. No, but it tells us—and shows us—that patience is possible even in the worst of circumstances that go on and on and on and on and on. In fact, faith is strong enough to carry us even through a lifetime of suffering, if that is what we must face. And we find, in the midst of it all, "the Lord is full of compassion and mercy" (James 5:11).

☞ God's Word says . . .

"Be patient" [How long?] "until the Lord's coming" (James 5:7).

☞ Make it a prayer . . .

Lord, give me the patience to face the little irritations and the big traumas, with faith.

The Fruit of the Spirit Is Patience

It's pretty amazing when you stop to think about it: Even God has to exercise patience.

☞ Think about it . . .

What stirs impatient feelings in God? What is it that he might like to hurry along? Well, what's going on right now that bothers him?

Human suffering and misery hurt the heart of God. Don't you think he would like to see our sorrow brought to an end? Our disappointment and frustration are felt by God. Can you see him eager to hurry things along to better times? He witnesses our inhumanity, a planet in rebellion against the excellence he has planned for it. And he weeps. Wouldn't God be anxious to usher in the best of all possible times?

Of course he would.

Instead, he is patient. He waits for people to turn from the things that would hurt them, to the only one who can truly help them.

Some day there will come an end to all that tries our patience, and all that tests the patience of God. Some day things will get unimaginably better. And we will celebrate forever, God and us.

☞ God's Word says . . .

"With the Lord a day is like a thousand years, and a thousand years are like a day. The Lord is not slow in keeping his promise, as some understand slowness. He is patient with you" (2 Peter 3:8–9).

☞ Make it a prayer . . .

Thank you, Lord, for being patient. Thank you, for showing us the way home, then waiting for us to turn and take that road.

The Fruit of the Spirit Is Patience

What would happen if the only thing you ever had to wait for was God? If the only thing that demanded your patience was someone who loved you, who ruled the universe, and who always had your best interests at heart, wouldn't patience come easier?

☞ Think about it . . .

We struggle with patience because we don't like the circumstances we are facing. Patience is difficult because things feel out of control. The timing seems wrong—the wait drags on and on. We would do things differently if we only had the power. Who finds it easy to be patient?

Here's a different way of looking at it. Because God is in control, I can be patient. Because God loves me, I can relax. Because God's wisdom is flawless, I can wait.

In a sense, the only thing I ever have to wait for is my God, who is in control. The only thing that ever demands my patience is the wise God who loves me. When I wait for circumstances to change, I wait for God to change those circumstances. When hardship tests my patience, it is the powerful, loving, wise God who will, in time, lift my burdens.

When I look at life from that perspective, I can finally be still and wait with patience for better things.

☞ God's Word says . . .

"Be still before the Lord and wait patiently for him"
(Psalm 37:7).

☞ Make it a prayer . . .

Thank you, Lord, for teaching me that patience means trust, and all I ever really wait for is you.

Week 6

The Fruit of the Spirit Is Kindness

KEY TO KINDNESS

Kindness is what gives love definition. Shape and form. I know what love looks like because I see your kindness.

Weekend Reading

Because he was the older brother of one of my best friends, I knew Gene fairly well. I remember my admiration being mixed with a little sadness as he packed up his old Volvo and left for college. I was just starting high school at the time. Suddenly I, like Gene's family and friends, looked forward to vacations a little more, knowing he'd be returning to his Southern California home from Fresno State.

What impressed me about him then and still does now is that I never once heard him make a critical remark about anyone. You'd think of Gene and words like "positive" would pop into your mind. You couldn't help it; he just had this upbeat air about him. He brought out the best in everyone he was around. People smiled more, said nice things more frequently, acted more sensitively, just because they were near him.

Through his positive attitude toward people, I learned something of what *kindness* means.

I also learned something about kindness from my own brother. He was two years older than I, and though I certainly wouldn't suggest that we did not often fight, I never doubted his loyalty to me. His protectiveness toward me. Even, I think, his pride in me.

I took up the drums at age twelve or thirteen, I don't recall exactly. But it became a major diversion for me; I practiced for hours on end. It wasn't long before I gathered a few neighborhood musicians and formed my first band. But I remember distinctly my brother's concern that I did not have better, more reliable equipment. It was my brother who replaced my snare drum with a classy (and costly) chrome Ludwig. Then he brought me a new hi-hat and Avedis Zildjian cymbals. It was his way of participating in his younger brother's interests. Further expression of his loyalty, his protectiveness, his pride.

Through that generosity and selflessness I learned a bit more about *kindness*.

I have felt kindness through a friend's simple question: "Jim, how's it going today?" Or through a teacher I respected telling me, "I think you'd be good at that." I have experienced kindness through my parents' forgiveness. Through a birthday card with just the right personal message. Through a girlfriend's smile. Through a touch. Through a rebuke that I needed to hear.

Now, as I sit here writing out these ideas on kindness, reflecting on the thoughtfulness of my family or my friends, I can so easily relive the heartening impact of kind words or thoughtful actions, even though they may have taken place years ago. Still they feel immediate, recent. There is such power in kindness. Power for good. Power to make me better. And if I am kind, power in me to make others better. Such kindness makes the strong statement that God can change people, and he can use people to change other people. All for the better.

Think about it, then. What *is* kindness? How do you nurture it? How do you unlock it and express it?

Let's say this, first and plainly:

Kindness conquers selfishness.

Perhaps this is obvious enough. Kindness is defined, in part, by that which it won't tolerate: self-centeredness.

Kindness and self-centeredness just don't enjoy one another's company. They are mutually exclusive. They fight one another. Invite kindness in the front door of your life, selfishness must leave by the back door. Or climb out the window. They don't go together.

We could say, somewhat negatively, selfishness strangles kindness until there is no life left in it. But couldn't we instead say: nurture kindness in your life and it will suffocate your self-centeredness?

Want to break out of your selfish ways (and we all have them)? Look for ways to express kindness.

You don't think of yourself as particularly egotistical, but do others? Give your life away in kindness to others and even the unacknowledged, unknown dimensions of your selfishness within will begin to melt away.

When we lose ourselves in kindness to others we become new people. Entirely new. Different. More likable. Pleasant to be around. Most likely with fewer enemies.

But what if we don't lose our enemies? What if there are those who don't like us or who oppose us? Then what?

Even then, express love in common kindness.

Jesus put it like this:

> *"You have heard that it was said, 'Love your neighbor and hate your enemy.' But I tell you: love your*

*enemies and pray for those who persecute you, that
you may be sons of your Father in heaven. He causes
his sun to rise on the evil and the good, and sends
rain on the righteous and the unrighteous. If you love
those who love you, what reward will you get? Are
not even the tax collectors doing that? And if you
greet only your brothers, what are you doing more
than others? Do not even pagans do that? Be perfect,
therefore, as your heavenly Father is perfect"*
(Matthew 5:43–48).

What is kindness like? It begins with this:

Kindness *feels* what others feel.

The joy, the sadness. The up times and the down
times. Kindness in me will celebrate along with others
when they feel good reason to celebrate. Kindness in
me will also feel the hurting inside others. It's as if it
takes ownership of a part of that hurt. Kindness begins
in me when I reach toward you and then come alongside to share what I now know you are feeling.

> *"Rejoice with those who rejoice; mourn with those
> who mourn. Live in harmony with one another"
> (Romans 12:15–16).*

But kindness is more than sharing a feeling.

Kindness in me meets needs in you.

It is active. Practical. We *see* kindness. It shows itself in
practical ways. It smiles. It offers encouraging words. It
tutors a student who needs the help. It mows a lawn or

shovels a sidewalk for an elderly neighbor. It compliments a parent. It shares with a brother or sister.

Kindness is helping out at a rest home, giving up a summer to build a schoolhouse in Haiti, setting aside a few bucks a month from that part-time job to sponsor a child through Compassion or Children's International.

Kindness is also gently warning a friend about a wrong direction they're taking, refusing to ridicule that one girl at school who is "different," deciding not to cheat on that test.

Kindness takes action.

> *"Suppose a brother or sister is without clothes and daily food. If one of you says to him, 'Go, I wish you well; keep warm and well fed,' but does nothing about his physical needs, what good is it?" (James 2:15–16).*

Words, then, without the helpful actions that should go with them, are empty. Even unkind.

Which is another way of saying:

Kindness is love expressing itself.

Kindness is what gives love definition. Shape and form. I know what love looks like because I see your kindness. We can say we care, that we have love. Whatever. But that's not love, that's just talk. It is kindness that proves love, because kindness is an outward, tangible expression of it.

If I am not kind, I am not loving.

> *"If anyone has material possessions and sees his brother in need but has no pity on him, how can the love of God be in him? Dear children, let us not love*

with words or tongue but with actions and in truth.
This then is how we know that we belong to the truth,
and how we set our hearts at rest in his presence"
(1 John 3:17–20).

I saw kindness in my brother not so much because he gave me things—and expensive things at that—but because I knew he was *feeling* with me. He was interested in me. He left self-centeredness behind. In a similar way, my friend's brother, Gene, was able to toss kindness around in every direction because he didn't let his own problems blind him to the needs of others. Or to life's positive side. He had broken free of pessimism and criticism, cynicism and sarcasm, and somehow found a way to see the good God was spreading through life.

It was kind of him to help the rest of us catch a glimpse of that good.

I thumbed through a Bible the other day, tracing out the idea of kindness. I found it used side by side with friendship and generosity. Hospitality and warmheartedness. Doing good and expressing love. Being helpful and showing sympathy. I saw kindness coupled with understanding, patience, courtesy, thoughtfulness, compassion, and forgiveness.

The Bible expresses the idea unmistakably: It is love that proves we have faith. Well, it is kindness that proves we have love.

"The fruit of the Spirit is ... kindness"
(Galatians 5:22).

The Fruit of the Spirit Is Kindness

We like others to be kind to us, but being kind to them can sometimes be a challenge. What stands in the way?

☞ Think about it . . .

It is amazing what happens when we rise to the challenge—when we take the bold step to show kindness to others. People appreciate our kindness and are often surprised by it. Sometimes our kindness reminds someone of Jesus. We all know kindness is a positive trait, we see the good it brings. So, what keeps us from freely expressing kindness toward others?

Sometimes we hold back kindness because we're selfish and just don't get around to thinking of others. We'd do kindness if we just remembered.

Other times we make a conscious choice to withhold kindness because someone has been unkind to us. You treat me crummy, I treat you crummy. But isn't it precisely when others have treated us the worst that we have the greatest opportunity to show kindness? Isn't this the sort of kindness Jesus expressed? Kindness even toward those who were unkind to him?

It's not surprising then, that the Bible links kindness and forgiveness. There are those times we could never express kindness unless we first practiced forgiveness.

☞ God's Word says . . .

"Be kind and compassionate to one another, forgiving each other, just as in Christ God forgave you" (Ephesians 4:32).

☞ Make it a prayer . . .

Lord, show me at least one opportunity today where I can express kindness, even toward those who are not so kind to me.

The Fruit of the Spirit Is Kindness

If kindness is so great, doing good things in us and in others, what aren't we more kind? Well, it's not hard to see what stands in our way. Why, *we* do, of course.

☞ Think about it . . .

We are our own worst enemy in so many ways. We stand between ourselves and what God wants to accomplish in us.

Kindness, for instance.

But what would happen if we simply practiced kindness whether we felt like it or not? Our kindness would conquer our selfishness.

Don't you suppose kindness is stronger than selfishness?

Try this: Brainstorm kindness. On a sheet of paper, list at least one expression of kindness for each of the following people — something you could do for that person this week. A parent, a brother or sister, a friend, an acquaintance (a neighbor or coworker, perhaps), a stranger, even an enemy. Can you predict what might happen if you took the time and made the effort to show kindness in this way? Write down your "prediction," give your gift of kindness, and see what happens.

☞ God's Word says . . .

"If you love those who love you, what reward will you get? Are not even the tax collectors doing that? And if you greet only your brothers, what are you doing more than others?"
(Matthew 5:46–47).

☞ Make it a prayer . . .

Help me, Lord, to take the initiative. To take the first bold step of kindness. Help me show kindness at home, among my friends, at school or work. Help me show kindness even toward strangers and enemies. Make me more like you.

The Fruit of the Spirit Is Kindness

Where does kindness begin? What revs it up and keeps it going?

☞ **Think about it . . .**

We might sometimes need to jump-start kindness. We might need to do something kind whether we feel like it or not. But sooner or later, true kindness touches our feelings. We *feel* what others feel, and it prompts kindness.

Take a personal inventory. Think of a parent, a brother or sister, a friend. Think of times you have seen that person happy or sad, excited or confused. How did their feelings make you feel?

The Bible urges us to feel happiness for those who are happy and to share in the sadness of those who are sad. The Bible says we ought to live "in harmony with one another." When our feelings are stirred by the feelings of others, living in harmony comes naturally.

This week, make an effort to notice the feelings of others. Ask yourself, what was my mom feeling when the car broke down? How did it make my sister feel when I yelled at her? How did my friend feel when he got the job? Then ask yourself, how can I let them know that I share in their feelings? Can I write a letter, make a call, pay a visit? What would I say? What would I do that would express my kind feelings?

☞ **God's Word says . . .**

"Rejoice with those who rejoice; mourn with those who mourn. Live in harmony with one another" (Romans 12:15–16).

☞ **Make it a prayer . . .**

Help me to feel what my friends feel. Open my heart to make room for others.

The Fruit of the Spirit Is Kindness

It isn't enough to *feel* kindness toward someone. Kindness proves itself in action.

☞ Think about it ...

There is great power in kindness. Power to make me better. Power to make better every life I touch. It may begin with how I feel, but those kind feelings need to be expressed in action.

Yes, kindness is active. It is also practical. Kindness does things.

I will start a list. Take out a sheet of paper and see how many things you can add to the list. What does kindness do? Kindness smiles. It says encouraging things. Kindness says "thank you" to a parent. It shares with a brother or sister. Kindness cuts the grass or shovels the snow for an elderly neighbor. Kindness warns a friend who's heading in the wrong direction. Kindness drives patiently and carefully. Okay, what else does kindness do? What would kindness do through you today? This week?

There are also things kindness refuses to do. Kindness won't gossip. It refuses to cheat. Kindness won't make fun of others; it won't insult them. Kindness doesn't have time to waste on pouting or jealousy. What would you add to the list? What does kindness avoid? Make some notes on a sheet of paper.

☞ God's Word says ...

"Suppose a brother or sister is without clothes and daily food. If one of you says to him, 'Go, I wish you well; keep warm and well fed,' but does nothing about his physical needs, what good is it?" (James 2:15–16).

☞ Make it a prayer ...

Lord, teach me what to do and what to avoid in order to be kind. Make me sensitive to your suggestions and impulses.

The Fruit of the Spirit Is Kindness

What *is* kindness? It is love showing its true colors.

☞ Think about it . . .

Love is invisible. Kindness brings it out in the open.

Love can't be seen. Kindness causes it to materialize.

Think about the love of a parent—your mom or dad. How do you know you are loved? Perhaps it is expressed in words, you hear it spoken, "I love you." But how has it been *shown* to you? What kinds of things do parents do because they love?

There is a connection between love and kindness.

Think about the care that friends have for one another. How is that expressed?

What about the person who has few friends? Who shows kindness to him or her? Who offers a hand when it's needed? Who speaks an encouraging word?

The Bible tells us that our expression of kindness—our love—is not something we horde and offer only to friends and family. Kindness is a gift we give to all in need. How would it change what you do today and tomorrow if you decided right now that you would spread this gift of kindness to all who needed it?

☞ God's Word says . . .

"If anyone has material possessions and sees his brother in need but has no pity on him, how can the love of God be in him? Dear children, let us not love with words or tongue but with actions and in truth. This then is how we know that we belong to the truth, and how we set our hearts at rest in his presence" (1 John 3:17–20).

☞ Make it a prayer . . .

Thank you, Lord, for your generosity. Thank you for expressing loving kindness to everyone, not just a favored few. Fill me, Lord, with kindness for others—for all who need encouragement and help.

Week 7

The Fruit of the Spirit Is Goodness

TREATING EVERYONE AS FRIEND

The idea of "being good" may sound boring. Actually, it is more like sharing the gift of friendship with the world.

Weekend Reading

If you could listen in as a friend described you to others, what would you like to hear?

Would you want your friend to mention your appearance or personality, your intelligence or sense of humor, your hobbies or achievements?

How about this description: "He goes around doing good."

It's a remarkable compliment, but some of us might be embarrassed to receive it. We might feel uneasy being called "good." As if "being good" isn't good. It sounds stuffy, boring. Too religious or moral. Some people laugh at the PTA or the Puritans or G-rated movies—images of "goodness." Some of us are just too sophisticated to feel comfortable with the label "good."

But I've been thinking of the "good" label in different terms. If a friend shows goodness toward us, we don't turn that goodness away. When a parent is fair with us, we don't resent it. Between friends and family, we welcome goodness. We even expect it. And in the context of friendship and family we freely express goodness in ourselves; we're not normally embarrassed to do what is good. One way to think of goodness, then, is to imagine everyone as friend and then treat them as such.

"Everyone's friend"—what a great label to earn!

Remembering his life and how he lived it, friends said of Jesus: "He went around doing good." Everything he touched he left better than it had been. Sick people discovered health. Lonely people encountered love. Guilty people found forgiveness.

He spread goodness generously everywhere, offering friendship to any who would accept it. In doing so, he gave us a supreme way to think of "goodness." What it is. What it's like. How it acts.

Goodness is something we do.

This is obvious enough. Kind or moral actions express good. We volunteer time for peer counseling. We mow lawns or shovel snow for the elderly. We include "outcasts" in our circle of friends. We forgive when wronged. We refuse to gossip. We resist doing anything that would tear down us or others. We share our money with people who need it. We are kind to our kid brother. We may even do the "religious" things others label as good—go to church, pray, read the Bible, point someone toward Jesus.

Jesus "went around doing good" (Acts 10:38).

We are told to do likewise. *"Do not forget to do good and to share with others, for with such sacrifices God is pleased" (Hebrews 13:16).* Sometimes spreading goodness to everyone truly is sacrificial. Sometimes it is very unpleasant to do good. Especially when someone treats us badly. But we read: *"Love [even] your enemies, do good [even] to those who hate you" (Luke 6:27).* And not only that, but *"anyone ... who knows the good he ought to do and doesn't do it, sins" (James 4:17).*

Goodness is something we do.

But where does this goodness come from?

Goodness is something we are.

It begins within us. In the core of who we are. *"The good man brings good things out of the good stored up in him,"* Jesus said (Matthew 12:35). We *do* good, because we *are* good.

That's how goodness ought to operate, at least. It doesn't always. We may instead do good because we are afraid of the consequences of doing bad. We are fearful of getting caught by our parents or by a teacher or by the law or by God. Or we manufacture an insincere brand of goodness because we want to impress someone—a friend, a parent, the church, God. So we put on a show, trying very hard to do the good that does not come to us naturally.

If that's our goodness, is it really good? It may produce good results, but can it honestly be called "good"?

Well, on one level, sure it is honestly good. Most of us try our best to be our best. Sincere effort should count for something. Our motives may be a bit mixed at times, but most of us are only occasionally aware that our goodness might not be fully good. Go ahead, call it "good."

On the other hand, though, is another standard by which we are measured. And the results are not so encouraging.

Goodness is something we aren't.

Our motives are so mixed, our lives so inconsistent, that though we may do some good, we are not as good as we want others to think we are. Or even, for that matter, as good as we think we are. In spite of our occasional and earnest attempts to do right, the Bible still says: *"There is no one who does good, not even one.... All have sinned and fall short of the glory of God"* (Romans 3:12, 23).

A depressing assessment.

How can the Bible say that? How can it picture even good people as so lacking in goodness?

The Bible is measuring us by a different standard.

It is interesting how Jesus responded when a certain rich man called him "good" (Luke 18:18–30).

"Why do you call me good?" he said. *"No one is good— except God alone."*

And the entire conversation that follows pivots on that one simple question and that one straightforward statement.

"Why do you call me good?"

"No one is good—except God alone."

The answer to the question ought to be: "Jesus, I call you 'good' because I recognize that you are God." The response to the statement ought to be: "Yes, Jesus, I realize that in the absolute sense—the sense that matters most—there is no one good except God alone. Now Jesus, please, make me good!"

Goodness is something we are given.

This is the truly astounding part: God will give me goodness deep down in the core of my character, even before I may appear "good" to others.

Now, before that can happen, I must first face my own lack of deep-down goodness. I am not good enough to please God. "All have sinned," and I'm part of the all. Sin carries a high price—a certain consequence—but Jesus, who was truly good, died to take the consequence for me. *"The wages of sin is death, but the gift of God is eternal life in Christ Jesus our Lord" (Romans 6:23).* Faith takes the gift; holds it and values it. Then goodness comes.

> *"God made him who had no sin to be sin for us, so that in him we might become the righteousness of God" (2 Corinthians 5:21).*

God sees me differently, as if he looks at me but now sees instead the character of Jesus. But it does not stop there. He also plants goodness like a seed deep into my character, and it begins to grow. I keep getting better, from the inside out.

Obviously, if you know me or know yourself, you recognize that the process of expressing this good is not instantaneous. It is, in fact, a long, slow struggle (see Romans 7). But though our growth in goodness is slow and painful, it is also certain. We shed our bad ways and wrong motives and live out our gift of goodness.

It can't be hidden for long.

Those closest to you see the change. Your family. Your friends. At some point they may even begin to think of you as the person who "goes around doing good."

When that happens, smile and thank the one who gave you goodness.

"The fruit of the Spirit is ... goodness"
(Galatians 5:22).

The Fruit of the Spirit Is Goodness

Suppose you walked into a crowded room, people looked up, and you heard someone quietly say your name. "There's Jeff, everybody's friend." Or "There's Molly—she's nice to everyone."

How would the compliment make you feel?

☞ Think about it ...

There are so many ways we could be described. "Yeah, he's the guy who lives in the gray house." "She aces every test—in every class." "You should hear him play the guitar!" "He looks great." "She's beautiful." "When he shoots free throws, he *always* makes at least nine out of ten." "He's so funny!" "Have you seen her car?"

But who wants to just be known for where they live, how much money their family makes, what they look like, what abilities they have, how smart they are, or how funny?

These things may be okay as far as they go, but to give a truly accurate description, people would have to look deeper than appearance or achievement or even just personality. What is your *character* like?

When people talked about Jesus, they said many things. One of the most interesting is this: "He went around doing good" (Acts 10:38). It was kind of like Jesus treated everyone like a friend. He had sharp words for hypocrites, of course. And he warned people about evil. But he first approached people like a friend—someone who needed the touch of goodness.

Now there's a goal!

☞ God's Word says ...

"Make every effort to add to your faith goodness"
(2 Peter 1:5).

☞ Make it a prayer ...

Give me the desire, Lord, to treat everyone as a friend—to go around doing good.

The Fruit of the Spirit Is Goodness

Want to make God happy? Do good and share with others, even when it's costly.

☞ Think about it ...

God is so great, it's easy to think of him as not needing or wanting anything from us. But that's not quite true. In fact, there are certain things we can do that even make him happy. When we do good to others, God is pleased. When we share, God is happy. Why is that? What is it about our doing good to people that puts a smile on God's face? Well, maybe it's because in doing good we are sharing in the very heartbeat of God. He loves people and is glad to meet their needs. When we treat people that way, we are sharing in his kind nature. No wonder it pleases him!

Goodness, then, is something we do. It is something we do for people that is similar to the kind things God would do for people. Goodness is expressing kindness. It is offering forgiveness. Lending a helping hand. Reaching out to the friendless.

Sometimes goodness is shown in something big and dramatic — acts of heroism, for instance. But every day we have many simple, common opportunities to give the gift of goodness.

Take out a sheet of paper and think about the good things others have done for you in the past few weeks. It may have been something as "small" as a pat on the back or an encouraging word. Try to identify at least ten ways others have been good to you recently. Think about today. How will you give the gift of goodness to others?

☞ God's Word says ...

"Do not forget to do good and to share with others, for with such sacrifices God is pleased" (Hebrews 13:16).

☞ Make it a prayer ...

Lord, show me ways I can please you today, by giving others the gift of goodness.

The Fruit of the Spirit Is Goodness

We all have secrets we'd just as soon keep hidden. But there's one secret about us that sooner or later will become apparent to anyone looking on, and that is, the "secret" of what we really are.

☞ Think about it . . .

It's possible to do good for the wrong reasons. That's why hypocrisy seems to work for a while. We can fool people. We can look Christian on the outside and still be pretty rotten on the inside.

Of course, God looks at us from the inside out. He isn't so impressed with what we do. He isn't snowed by what shows on the outside. He starts at our heart and works his way out from there. But life has a way of turning us inside out too. If people look at us long enough, they too most often will start to see right into our heart. And it is in the heart that true goodness begins. Goodness is something we do, yes. But it is first something that we are.

No one sees your heart quite so clearly as God does. But the person with the next best view, is you. You see your heart. Right now, take a long, honest look. What do you see inside? What do you see that's good, and what do you see that's not so good? Can you discuss it honestly with the God who sees it all anyway?

☞ God's Word says . . .

"The good man brings good things out of the good stored up in him" (Matthew 12:35).

☞ Make it a prayer . . .

Lord, you see me from the inside out and love me anyway. Make me honest with you about my strengths and weaknesses—those things that are good, and those that are evil.

The Fruit of the Spirit Is Goodness

Would God deliberately frustrate you? Would he do something that he knew before hand would drive you nuts? Well, yes, if doing so would do you good.

☞ Think about it . . .

God *has* done something to frustrate us. He has done something to drive us nuts. God has held up a standard he knew we couldn't meet. He's given us laws he knew we would break. He's held up a mirror that shows us our soul. He's allowed us to see the limits of our goodness. When we compare ourselves to the goodness of God and to the goodness of his law, we fall short. In fact, we fall so far short we don't even look good at all.

We might think of all those good things we do, and suddenly we see that many of those good things were done for the wrong reasons. Maybe we did good things to try and make people think we were better than we really are. Maybe we did good things but then felt so proud of ourselves that the goodness was almost outweighed by the pride it caused.

God has a dream for us. It is his dream that our goodness would be like his. Generous and humble and pure. It is his dream for us that we would do good because we *are* good and because we love what is good, not just because we're afraid of the consequences if we aren't good. Is his dream starting to come true in you?

☞ God's Word says . . .

"There is no one who does good, not even one. . . . All have sinned and fall short of the glory of God" (Romans 3:12, 23).

☞ Make it a prayer . . .

Show me what I am, Lord, and make me what you want me to be.

✓ Friday Checkpoint:

The Fruit of the Spirit Is Goodness

Isn't it just like God to give us the one thing we most desperately need?

☞ Think about it . . .

If God were not so generous, we would lack the one thing that could change us: goodness. If God did not intervene, we could never be good enough in the eyes of the one who matters most, in the estimation of the only one who ultimately matters at all: him. If God did not make us good, we could never be good enough on our own.

This is what is truly amazing about your faith. Your faith makes you good in the eyes of God. Your faith also reshapes your character. In time, faith makes you good.

In time.

It does take time. We can all identify with the guy who said, "What I want to do I do not do, but what I hate I do" (Romans 7:15). We all have this conflict within us. We try to measure up to our own idea of goodness—and maybe God's idea of goodness too. And we get frustrated. But God has started a process within us, and he won't quit.

We shouldn't either.

Read the verse that follows, then ask yourself: "What can I do differently today—how can I cooperate with the Spirit of God—so that people will look at me, and see even a glimpse of the righteousness of God?"

☞ God's Word says . . .

"God made him who had no sin to be sin for us, so that in him we might become the righteousness of God" (2 Corinthians 5:21).

☞ Make it a prayer . . .

Thank you, Lord, for the gift of goodness. Do the kind of work inside me that would cause people to say, "That person is just like Jesus. He goes around doing good."

Week *8*

The Fruit of the Spirit Is Faithfulness

I SAID IT, I'LL DO IT

There are many ways to prove we are different, better than we used to be. But few of them are more challenging than this . . .

Weekend Reading

It's a remarkable thing, really, to think that people can meet you and get to know you and, through you, be reminded of Jesus. Not that you would have a sandals-and-robe-and-halo kind of resemblance. Not even that religious words would drip from you like maple syrup. No, the remarkable thing is this: what we are on the inside can begin to take the shape of what Jesus was on the inside. Our character can become more and more like his.

If you know anything about Jesus, you know that this is very good news.

Now, if someone asked us, "Would you like to be religious?" we might hesitate. Some of the images religion brings to mind may not be appealing. We'd feel differently if the question were: "Would you like to know the secret of really loving? Would you like to be able to forgive? Would you like to overcome your worry? Would you like to be a better friend?"

Well, you could say—fairly, I think—that Christianity has less to do with being religious than learning to love and to forgive, learning to overcome worry and to express friendship.

In other words, Christianity is learning to be like Jesus.

Faith means I resemble him. I live in such a way as to remind other people of him.

We can learn to love less selfishly. We can astonish our friends, our parents, a brother or sister by becoming altogether new, with a deeper capacity to forgive when we are wronged. We can become more patient, not so easily agitated when things do not go our way. We can find an inner calmness, even when we have good reason to worry. We can express kindness consistently, and in doing so become the kind of friend to others that we want them to be to us.

This process of becoming like Jesus is described in different ways. Here's one example: *"The fruit of the Spirit* [what God causes to grow inside us] *is love, joy, peace, patience, kindness, goodness, faithfulness, gentleness and self-control" (Galatians 5:22–23).*

As I skim the list, I can make sense out of most of these words, but I pause on "faithfulness."

What does it mean that God will make me "faithful?"

Why does faithfulness matter? In what way will I look more like Jesus if I am more "faithful?"

I recall one of the first weddings I ever attended. A friend a few years older than I was marrying. He and his girlfriend had gone together for a couple of years. As their relationship had unfolded, they naturally shared more of their lives with each other. They discussed their dreams and hopes and fears. They began to talk a bit less in the first person singular—"I"—and more in the first person plural—"we." Their commitment deepened. In time they decided on a "shared future." He asked, "Will you?" She said, "Yes."

One summer Saturday afternoon a couple hundred friends and family members gathered at a church. As sunlight filtered through stained glass and organ music echoed off ceiling and walls, two friends vowed to share life. For better or worse. Richer. Poorer. Sickness. Health. They promised to pool their resources. To marry and stay married. To reserve love and affection for each other only. They promised "before God and these witnesses" to be faithful to each other.

It's not that difficult, then, to understand "faithfulness."

Faithfulness means: "I said it. I'll do it."

It means: "I will keep my word."

It means: "My words and my actions will always agree."

One day Jesus walked up a hillside, followed by his friends. He sat down and began to speak. As he did, a crowd gathered, listening, astonished at what he had to say and how he expressed it. He described, for instance, a different way to happiness—through mourning and meekness, persecution and purity. He spoke of his friends as "the light of the world," shining for all to see, through the good that they would do.

As you read what he said (Matthew 5–7), you can picture the confused expressions on people's faces as he told them that anger and murder were much alike; that lust and adultery were practically the same, that they should (of all things) love their enemies, doing good to those who hurt them. And he gave them reasons why they need worry about nothing.

"You can build your life on my words," he finally told them. "And if you do, your life will stand against anything. But if you build your life on anything less," he warned them, "it will collapse in a heap of rubble when hard times come."

These are all big ideas. Things that matter. But in the middle of the talk, Jesus made an issue of something that seems so small by comparison. He told them this: *"You have heard that it was said to the people long ago, 'Do not break your oath, but keep the oaths you have made to the Lord.' But I tell you, Do not swear at all. . . . Simply let your 'Yes' be 'Yes,' and your 'No,' 'No'; anything beyond this comes from the evil one"* (5:35–37).

Those who listened on that hillside understood. When they wanted to stress that their words were truthful, they would "swear it was true." Sort of like what we do in a courtroom: one hand on a Bible, the other raised as we must answer, "Do you swear that the testimony you are about to give is the truth, the whole truth, and nothing but the truth, so help you God?" Or sort of like the vows we make at weddings, "before God and these witnesses," sealing the promise with a token of our commitment: rings.

Jesus startled people by insisting that every single word, however small, must carry the weight of a solemn vow. "Yes" means "yes," not "maybe," or "if it's convenient." "No" means "no." Period.

This, then, is the core of faithfulness as Jesus expressed it.

Words must mean something.

What we say must always agree with our actions.

"I did my own work on the semester project; I did not cheat."

"I will be home by 11:00."

"I will call you on Saturday."

"I finished my homework."

"I will not repeat to others the secret you are trusting to me."

"Jesus, I will live for you alone."

Faithfulness means truthfulness. Words matter. They agree with what I do.

"I said it. I'll do it."

God is to us the supreme example of this sort of agreement between words and actions. Some people read the Bible as dusty history and find it boring. But read more attentively and you find that it is a record of God doing precisely what he said he would do. As King David celebrated it: "Great is your love, reaching to the heavens; your faithfulness reaches to the skies" (Psalm 57:10). The stories of the Bible, taken together, form a gallery, filled with portraits of God's faithfulness—a character trait we are asked to copy.

God says it. God does it.

Our words and actions must likewise agree.

It's not surprising, then, that Jesus urged those who would follow him to "count the cost." "If you're going to build a tower," he advised, "calculate the expense before you lay the foundation. If you are going to go to war, consider the odds. If you're going to follow me, living life as I insist it must be lived, be sure you know what you're signing up for. Be sure you're willing to follow through. Be sure your words mean something. Be sure you're prepared to be faithful—in the big things, and in the things that seem ridiculously insignificant."

Jesus wants more from us than mere religion.

He wants us to resemble him.

To live in such a way as to remind people of him.

That implies a lot of things: learning to love less selfishly. Finding a deeper capacity to forgive. Developing patience. Putting our worry to rest. Expressing kindness consistently.

But this also gives us the appearance of Jesus himself: *faithfulness.*

We say it.

We do it.

"The fruit of the Spirit is ... faithfulness"
(Galatians 5:22).

The Fruit of the Spirit Is Faithfulness

Could any greater compliment be given than this: "You remind me of Jesus"?

☞ **Think about it . . .**

Flip back a few pages to the beginning of this chapter. It was launched with this idea: Wouldn't you like to be like Jesus? What we are on the inside can begin to take the shape of what Jesus was on the inside. Our character can become more and more like his. Jesus knew the secret of loving, and so can you. He knew how to forgive, how to overcome worry, how to win against temptation, how to remain patient and calm in the face of irritation, how to be a better friend. And so can you.

In fact, you can take a snapshot of your life right now and compare it to a picture of Christ. Take out a sheet of paper and list the nine character traits discussed in this book and mentioned in the following verse. This is not just a list of character traits God is developing in your life, it is also the image of Jesus, who was perfect in each area. Ask yourself how you're doing. Give yourself a score between one and ten, ten being excellent. Which of these characteristics needs more of your attention right now?

Now focus your attention specifically on "faithfulness." What would it mean to you to be "more faithful" to God? What would it mean to be a more faithful friend? Or employee? Or student? In each of these relationships, how would you complete this phrase: "Faithfulness is when . . ."?

☞ **God's Word says . . .**

"The fruit of the Spirit is love, joy, peace, patience, kindness, goodness, faithfulness, gentleness and self-control" (Galatians 5:22–23).

☞ **Make it a prayer . . .**

Lord, you have started something truly good—making me more like Jesus. Would you give me the encouragement of seeing progress this week?

The Fruit of the Spirit Is Faithfulness

The bride stands facing the groom. The man looks into the woman's eyes. Individually, they have each made a decision. Together, they both now openly confess it. A public commitment is made, expressed in vows: "We will be faithful."

☞ Think about it . . .

Faithfulness means, I will keep my promises. I will honor my commitments. My word will *mean* something. If I say it, I will do it.

This is easy to understand as we think of those promises made at a wedding. Most of us have also seen those sacred promises broken.

But now, imagine this: What if our every promise carried something of the weight of a vow, a commitment not easily broken? What if our words could be taken at face value, as if they were a contract?

Think for a moment about your commitments, the promises you make. How faithful are you? What kind of reputation do you have? How dependable is your word?

Make it more specific. Can your parents count on your word? Are you where you say you will be? Do you return when you say you will return? If you agree to do a job, do you do it, just as you said you would?

Does your boss find you to be dependable? Do you complete school assignments on time? If you tell a friend you will do something, do you keep your commitment? If you make a promise to God, do you follow through? How are you doing in the area of faithfulness?

☞ God's Word says . . .

"Those who have been given a trust must prove faithful" (1 Corinthians 4:2).

☞ Make it a prayer . . .

Make me a person of my word, absolutely dependable, resolutely faithful.

The Fruit of the Spirit Is Faithfulness

Suppose you knew ahead of time that there was a way to build your life that is so reliable it would not fail. A foundation so stable that your life could rest on it without wavering.

☞ Think about it . . .

If you knew a certain way to successful life, wouldn't you pay attention to every detail? Wouldn't you follow it with great care?

Imagine yourself in the crowd following Jesus. You are impressed by his kindness and amazed by his words. As you follow him, he walks up the side of a hill and sits down. A hush falls over the crowd as they hang on every word. And you do the same. You can tell something significant is happening as you listen.

When he finishes what he has to say, he assures you that his words are so certain that you could build your life on them. If you follow his words and follow them carefully, destruction might sweep others away, but it will not touch you. And you believe him.

Later that evening, his words are still ringing in you ears. It is important to you that not one of them be forgotten. They are too important. These are words to live by. If you neglect them, you will regret it.

It was in this context that Jesus said we must be faithful. Our words must have meaning behind them. Our promises must be kept. If we give our word, we do what we say. We are predictably faithful in all our commitments.

☞ God's Word says . . .

"Let your 'Yes' be 'Yes,' and your 'No,' 'No'; anything beyond this comes from the evil one" (Matthew 5:37).

☞ Make it a prayer . . .

Lord, teach me the importance of faithfulness today, even in the littlest of things.

The Fruit of the Spirit Is Faithfulness

Think of all the people—thousands and thousands of them—who have followed God their whole lives long, from youth to old age. What could possibly cause them to keep following the ways of God?

☞ Think about it . . .

What could possibly cause people to keep following the ways of God? They find that he is faithful. His word can be counted on. He keeps his commitments. He does what he says he will do. His words and his actions agree. His word is as dependable as his love, and his love is as certain as his word.

We are considering the word *faithfulness*. It is a word that must describe us. In all of our relationships, we must be people who are faithful. We must keep our commitments to parents, to friends, to teachers, to employers.

What does it mean to be faithful? We can consider wedding vows, and remind ourselves that our every word should be as dependable as the most sacred and binding of promises.

What does it mean to be faithful? It means I measure my words as God himself measures his. I value my promises as God values his. I care about my commitments as God cares about his. I dare not treat words lightly. I don't make promises flippantly. I regard my commitments as binding.

What I say carries the weight of a contract.

☞ God's Word says . . .

"Great is your love, reaching to the heavens; your faithfulness reaches to the skies" (Psalm 57:10).

☞ Make it a prayer . . .

Lord, teach me to give my word only carefully, and to keep it absolutely.

The Fruit of the Spirit Is Faithfulness

If you knew your faith was going to be difficult, would you still follow God? If you knew Christianity was going to cost you something, would you still believe?

☞ Think about it . . .

We must be faithful in all of our commitments, but is there any commitment more important than the commitment we make to Christ? Particularly those promises we make to God cannot be taken lightly.

Jesus told his friends, "If you are going to start a building project, calculate the cost before you ever begin." If a grandiose plan is all you want, don't bother with the building. Just *talk* about building. Hold up an artist's conception or an architect's blue print, and talk, talk, talk. But if you plan to build, *plan*, then follow through with the plan.

Jesus told his friends, "This faithfulness thing is sort of like a military strategist. You don't go to war casually, without thought of the cost." No, you analyze the risk involved. Don't begin the enterprise unless you plan to finish it.

It's easy to toss around God words. "I trust you." "I love you." "I'm going to follow you, no matter what."

But will you be faithful in the commitment? Will the words mean something? Have you counted the cost?

God wants us to be characterized by faithfulness. Every commitment must carry the weight of a solemn, legally binding promise. But no commitment is more crucial than this one. No one is more deserving of our faithfulness than our God.

☞ God's Word says . . .

"If anyone would come after me, he must deny himself and take up his cross and follow me" (Mark 8:34).

☞ Make it a prayer . . .

By your grace, Lord, I will be faithful in my life-long commitment to you.

Week 9

The Fruit of the Spirit Is Gentleness

OPPOSITES ATTRACT

What is it? It has been known to bring people together as friends. It draws people—pulls them toward us. It may not be second-nature to us, but it can be developed. Discover friendship-power through the mystery of gentleness.

Weekend Reading

When I first met him, I thought of him as the Ultimate Friend. Sort of a Super Friend who always has the right word, the caring action, the something extra that attracts all kinds of people in all kinds of situations.

There was something in the way this Super Friend reacted to the unpopular people, for instance. The outsiders. Most of us worry that if we're too kind to "those weird people," we'll get labeled "weird" along with them. He didn't worry about that. If people needed friendship, he offered it.

It also amazed me to see how this Ultimate Friend treated depressed people. Self-destructive people. Most of us find it hard to tolerate those who are always down or discouraged. Maybe we muster a little kindness at times, but given the choice, we tend to head the other way. We avoid the problems of others, lest their sadness overwhelm us. But he made time for the troubled, as if it were his job to help carry their concerns.

I watched him closely, noting how he reacted when people offended him. Or made the same mistakes over and over. When someone hurts me, I lose patience quickly. Forgiveness is a struggle. He was different, passing out forgiveness freely, as if it cost him nothing. But I knew it really cost him everything.

Perhaps you've concluded that the Super Friend I'm writing about is Jesus Christ. But couldn't it also be you?

Opposites attract.

And people were attracted to Jesus because of a character trait of his that is so opposite of our character: he was gentle, as if it were second-nature. *We* must work at it.

I've been giving all this some thought, and I have concluded that there is tremendous friendship-power waiting to be discovered in the mystery of gentleness. Maybe if we could capture something of the gentleness that made Jesus the Ultimate Friend, maybe if we were a bit more like him, the change that would sweep through us would even touch our friendships.

These thoughts made me want to take a closer look at the mystery of gentleness. Here's what I found:

Gentleness is the signature of God, and should be our signature as well.

I recall the story of a man on the run. He had been bold and outspoken standing up to evil people in high places of leadership. Then came the death threats. And this guy, Elijah, took off to hide in the wilderness, deeply depressed.

He desperately needed encouragement. A sense that he had been on the right track. Assurance that he wasn't alone. God seemed remote. When so discouraged, how was he to "visualize" this unseen friend? If only Elijah could look at God eyeball to eyeball....

Not possible. But God did give him a demonstration. As the man stood on a mountainside, this is what he experienced:

*"A great and powerful wind tore the mountains
apart and shattered the rocks before the Lord, but the
Lord was not in the wind. After the wind there was
an earthquake, but the Lord was not in the earthquake. After the earthquake came a fire, but the Lord
was not in the fire. And after the fire came a gentle
whisper. When Elijah heard it, he pulled his cloak
over his face and went out and stood at the mouth of
the cave" (1 Kings 19:11–13).*

What followed was a conversation that Elijah found
most encouraging. God can display awesome power,
but it is his gentleness that draws us. Gentleness is his
signature. It should be ours as well.

"Let your gentleness be evident to all," the Bible says
(Philippians 4:5). Don't hide it. Don't withhold it.
Don't obscure it with the fire of anger or the wind of
opinion. Anyone ought to be able to see our gentleness. It ought to be our signature, clearly read in our
kind and caring spirit.

Gentleness is one of the first chapters in the autobiography of Christ.

I was curious. How does Jesus describe himself?

He could say: "I am wise and powerful." It would be
true, not necessarily a boast. Instead, he describes himself like this: *"I am gentle and humble in heart"*
(Matthew 11:29).

He urged anyone who was willing: *"Come to me, all you
who are weary and burdened, and I will give you rest"*
(11:28).

Many people—weary, burdened, discouraged—did come to him. Did find rest. What drew them to him? What made them dare to take steps toward one so perfect when they knew themselves to be so imperfect? What was the attractiveness of Jesus?

His gentleness.

There is a trend in fashion photography—also shows up sometimes in advertising and rock videos. Rock stars love it. It is that cold, hard, jaded, cynical look. The look that says, "You can tell I'm cool because I've been emptied of emotion." I don't think Jesus would fit into that trendy mold. I get the impression that to look into *his* eyes was to see love and patience and forgiveness.

And gentleness.

And I wonder, *What do people see when they look at me? Would I dare describe myself as he did: "I am gentle and humble in heart"? Or would it just embarrass me to be so unlike all those rock stars and flashy models?*

Gentleness is an unexpected super-power.

Here's the twist: while gentleness appears so soft, it is actually quite powerful. Flip through the book of Proverbs, for example, and you find that gentleness defuses anger; it turns away wrath (15:1). I've seen this happen. Respond to an angry person with angry words and the problem gets worse—quickly. Respond instead with gentleness and your calm tends to take away the anger.

The New Testament pictures gentleness as an antidote to violence and quarreling (1 Timothy 3:3). Some people fuss and fight, argue and bicker. It would be easy to be swept along with the fury. Except we know that the greater power lies with a gentle spirit. Power to transform individuals, even history itself.

When Jesus entered Jerusalem, it was not as a great general, wielding force. Instead, he sat on a donkey's colt, just as it had been predicted:

> *"See, your king comes to you, righteous and having salvation, gentle and riding on a donkey, on a colt, the foal of a donkey" (Zechariah 9:9).*

As that week unfolded he faced insult, hatred and violence. He did not retaliate. Even in the face of death he expressed gentleness.

And he changed the world.

Gentleness is a mark of excellence.

It is a mark of unfading attractiveness. That is, it attracts and keeps on attracting. It drew people to Jesus; it draws people to us. You read the Bible and find lots of talk on character—what we ought to be like. Throughout the lists, gentleness keeps recurring, as if it is a priority item on the self-improvement agenda God has for us. It is linked with humbleness and patience and respect and kindness and meekness and love as key to what we are to become.

Because, if I am to be like Jesus, the Ultimate Friend, I must learn the mystery of gentleness. It may be the opposite of what I am now, but it is an opposite others will find irresistibly attractive.

"The fruit of the Spirit is . . . gentleness"
(Galatians 5:23).

The Fruit of the Spirit Is Gentleness

Gentleness only appears soft. Actually, it is quite powerful, overcoming anger, for instance, with its quiet strength.

☞ Think about it . . .

Think of Jesus. What was it that drew people to him? Why were they so impressed that they would drop everything to follow him? They could tell there was truth in what he said. They could also *see* that truth in him.

For months and months, Jesus' friends were with him. They walked with him, talked with him, ate with him. They saw how he reacted when he was tired. They saw how he handled anger. They saw his compassion for the sick and his tenderness with children. They noticed how he responded to growing rejection.

Turn the image around. What did Jesus see when he looked at his friends? He saw individuals with shortcomings and potential, people in need of the hand of God. And each one was different. Different backgrounds, different personalities. Yet they all felt drawn to Jesus. What was it about him that attracted all kinds of people—the young, the old, the rich, the poor, the educated, the simple, the strong, the weak?

Was it his gentleness? His kindness? His unmistakable love?

What if we could capture something of the gentleness that made Jesus the ultimate friend? What if we were a bit more like him? The change that would sweep through us would touch even our friendships.

☞ God's Word says . . .

"I have called you friends, for everything that I learned from my Father I have made known to you" (John 15:15).

☞ Make it a prayer . . .

Give me, Lord, the friendship power of Jesus—his gentle kindness.

The Fruit of the Spirit Is Gentleness

If I say, "Picture God," what do you see? If I say, "Imagine the Almighty God," what comes to mind?

☞ Think about it ...

Elijah was discouraged. Things were not going as he had anticipated and he needed some direct word from God. His sagging spirits needed a lift. What did he expect to see? What did he anticipate hearing?

Did he expect a great and destructive wind? A powerful jarring earthquake? A blazing inferno? God's voice was not in the wind; not in the earthquake; not in the fire. God's voice came to Elijah in a gentle whisper.

There is no question that God is almighty. He can speak through the wind; the Lord answered Job out of the storm (Job 38:1). He might speak through the earthquake; he promises to shake the heavens and the earth, the sea and dry land (Haggai 2:6). He can raise his voice through the purifying fire, as he spoke to Moses out of a burning bush (Exodus 3:4).

But sometimes it is the gentle whisper that most expresses the voice of God. And, like God, sometimes it is our moments of gentleness that are the greatest displays of our strength.

☞ God's Word says ...

"The Lord said, 'Go out and stand on the mountain in the presence of the Lord, for the Lord is about to pass by.' ... After the fire came a gentle whisper. When Elijah heard it, he pulled his cloak over his face and went out and stood at the mouth of the cave" (1 Kings 19:11, 12–13).

☞ Make it a prayer ...

Lord, teach me to show my strength in gentleness.

The Fruit of the Spirit Is Gentleness

If someone said, "Describe yourself," how would you respond? Think about the real, deep down inside *you*. What are you like?

☞ Think about it . . .

When Jesus wanted to describe himself, he said, "I am gentle and humble in heart." He wanted to encourage stressed-out and weary people to bring all their cares to him. He promised, if they did, they would find rest.

Don't miss the surprise in his words. "Give me your cares, and I will give *you* rest. I am gentle." He is gentle, but strong enough to carry our concerns. Gentleness, you see, is quite powerful. It is strength under control. Gracefulness of spirit.

Some of us would be embarrassed to be thought of as gentle. It sounds so weak. But is it? When God represents himself as gentle, he presents it as a strength. When Jesus describes himself as gentle, it is to show us he is understanding and has the strength to carry our concerns.

For us too there are times when the greatest display of strength is an expression of gentleness. A sensitive word to a concerned friend. An understanding look when a parent faces hardship. An act of kindness toward a grandparent. A helping hand for a child. Like Jesus, we will find that the time for the greatest display of gentleness is when we are stretching out a helping hand to someone who needs us. Someone who is counting on our strength.

☞ God's Word says . . .

"I am gentle and humble in heart" (Matthew 11:29).

☞ Make it a prayer . . .

Make me kind enough and caring enough to treat people with tenderness. Make me gentle enough to be strong for a friend who needs me.

The Fruit of the Spirit Is Gentleness

What has the power to diffuse anger, calm violence, and bring peacefulness to quarreling parties? It's not *force*. It's *gentleness*.

☞ Think about it . . .

You're walking across campus and are confronted by someone you know only casually. He is angry and is wrongfully accusing you of something. He's irrational, and it makes you angry. Your inclination is to lash out at him, as he has lashed out at you. But experience has taught you that anger only increases anger. What you need instead is the strength to be gentle and calm.

Proverbs, the Old Testament handbook of wisdom, makes the point. Harsh words inflame; gentle words calm.

Paul knew that misunderstanding and even violence can erupt among people who claim to be Christian. People may fight and fuss, argue and bicker. How do you respond without getting swept up in the fray? Be gentle (1 Timothy 3:3).

If you have ever stood face-to-face with a very angry individual, you know that it requires great strength of character to respond with gentleness.

Jesus gave us a powerful example the last week of his life when he rode into a city controlled by his enemies, not on a white charger, ready for battle. No, it had been predicted that the king would come, "gentle and riding on a donkey, on a colt" (Zechariah 9:9).

☞ God's Word says . . .

"A gentle answer turns away wrath, but a harsh word stirs up anger" (Proverbs 15:1).

☞ Make it a prayer . . .

As I face anger and conflict this week, remind me of the power of a gentle answer.

☑ Friday Checkpoint:

The Fruit of the Spirit Is Gentleness

Gentleness may be the opposite of what you are now, but it is an opposite others will find irresistibly attractive.

☞ Think about it . . .

Remember: The gentleness of Jesus was the magnet that drew people to him. It astounded them. How could anyone have such strength?

It is the strength of gentleness that calms anger and agitation. A quiet answer, not a forceful, rowdy response.

You have to feel rather self-confident to be gentle. Insecure people are more inclined to put on an outward show of strength.

Over and over again, God points to gentleness as one of the character traits he wants to form within us. To be like Jesus, is to be gentle. When we are, we will find one of the great mysteries of friendship opening before us. People are drawn by our gentleness. It makes them appreciative of our help, and curious about our inner strength.

☞ God's Word says . . .

"As God's chosen people, holy and dearly loved, clothe your-selves with compassion, kindness, humility, gentleness and patience. Bear with each other and forgive whatever griev-ances you may have against one another. Forgive as the Lord forgave you. And over all these virtues put on love" (Colos-sians 3:12–14).

☞ Make it a prayer . . .

Lord, write this verse in my life. Make me compassionate, kind, humble, gentle and patient. Teach me to forgive. Plant your love within me. Make me the kind of friend people found in Jesus, who called himself "gentle."

Week 10

The Fruit of the Spirit Is Self-control

I AM WHAT I FOLLOW

My life changed completely when I opened up to God, and everyone agreed: The changes made me better. But I soon discovered this was only a beginning. I had to learn to control "me."

Weekend Reading

What I remember most clearly is feeling clean. I knew I was starting over, and that everything in my past would stay there, buried under an avalanche of God's love and forgiving forgetfulness. This was more than a vague religious experience; of that I was certain. My life had changed. I had made a U-turn to follow a different way. How could I ever turn back?

My language changed.

The way I treated people improved.

I found I could more easily forgive those who had hurt me.

Things I'd valued lost their importance as better things took their place.

I felt forgiven, invited by God to start over, clean every day.

Then I fell.

I lost my temper with my father. As the disagreement got out of hand, I knew I was being unkind; I could feel myself turning in that direction. Yet I did not care enough to turn back. After all, I had a legitimate point. Good reason to be angry. The argument did not last long, but as I think on it now, I remember clearly how dirty I felt inside. I had started a new life, and the newness had lasted a mere two weeks.

Over the months that followed, I often felt I was failing as a new Christian. It wasn't just anger, either.

There were other moral struggles as well. I allowed those struggles to overshadow the good changes that were taking place.

It is deeply frustrating to decide to be a different person and then to find that your best efforts at self-improvement are not good enough. I was somewhat reassured to discover that one of the guys who helped write the Bible felt the same way. He said: *"I have the desire to do what is good, but I cannot carry it out. . . . When I want to do good, evil is right there with me"* (Romans 7:18, 21).

Yet this same writer, Paul, didn't stop there. He didn't dwell on the negative, like I had. He also talked about positive changes that come to those who know God personally. God's Spirit would take charge, he said, directing a new beginning. His mark would be seen on us. In our character.

> *"The fruit of the Spirit is love, joy, peace, patience, kindness, goodness, faithfulness, gentleness and self-control"* (Galatians 5:22–23).

As I read that and then thought about life, I could see that I had begun to experience these changes. But that last quality, self-control, is what seemed so elusive. If I could just learn self-control . . . If I could just keep the improvements coming . . .

This was what I needed: some sort of key to make the whole process work. That key, I felt, would have to be self-control. Without it, the good changes would soon dwindle away.

But what exactly is self-control? And how does a person get it?

Self-control means: I control "me."

It does require effort. The good that I want to see in me will not happen apart from my effort. God and I are in partnership in a great enterprise: making me better. I must do my part.

On the other hand . . .

Self-control begins when I see that I cannot control me.

My best efforts, unaided by God, are bound to fail. I will probably achieve some improvement; trying to be good does not generally lead to someone being worse. But the higher I set my standards for moral improvement, the greater my disappointment and discouragement. Self-control is just too big a job for me to handle alone.

Self-control happens when I let God control me.

This sounds quite mystical, and in some sense it is. I am certain that God is doing something in me that escapes my awareness. Maybe I see it only later, as I look back and realize that I have progressed.

Jesus once used an example from agriculture. He said that it is as if he is a vine and we are branches, drawing life and nourishment from him (John 15:5). Or, as it is expressed elsewhere, *"He who began a good work in*

you will carry it on to completion" (Philippians 1:6).
God is at work in me. He will not grow discouraged
with the process. He will not give up and quit.

Self-control happens when I get out of the way and let
God have his way with me. And yet, self-control is still
self-control. Without my involvement, the changes will
not come.

Here, in one statement from the Bible, are both sides of
the paradox: *"Continue to work out your salvation with
fear and trembling, for it is God who works in you to will
and to act according to his good purpose"* (Philippians
2:12–13).

I can work, because he works.

As I think back on that angry outburst with my dad or
any one of my other moral failures, I can see what
could have been done differently. I can ask myself, *If I
had exercised self-control, what would I have done? And
how would it have improved the outcome?*

I could, for instance, have seen things from my father's
perspective. Or I could have waited for a less emotional time to discuss my viewpoint.

It now seems to me that every time I have made a
wrong moral choice, a better alternative was right
there, waiting to be chosen by me.

> *"No temptation has seized you except what is com-
> mon to man. And God is faithful; he will not let you
> be tempted beyond what you can bear. But when you*

*are tempted, he will also provide a way out so that
you can stand up under it" (1 Corinthians 10:13).*

No temptation is too strong.

Self-control is not out of reach.

I am what I follow.

Self-control also has something to do with what I call
myself. My label, as it were. I say that I am a Christian, but the name has lost much of its meaning. It
has become so commonplace that I easily forget its
meaning.

What is a Christian? A disciple, or follower of Jesus.
Christians used to call themselves "Followers of the
Way," meaning that they intended to live life as Jesus
lived it, and they would act in each situation as Jesus
taught them to act.

Then you uncover this little phrase in the Bible: *"The
disciples were called Christians first at Antioch" (Acts
11:26).* This new name, "Christian," which was meant
to "link" a person to Christ, actually started out as a
way to ridicule a follower of Jesus. It was the ultimate
insult, a bit like saying, "You're so weird you live like
Christ."

Ironically, these followers of Jesus took it as a
compliment.

So should we.

When I call myself "Christian," I mean that I live as
Christ lived.

When I get angry at my father and am tempted to throw away my self-control, I ask myself, "How would Christ respond?" When I face great moral temptation and I want badly to give in, I remind myself that I share the name of Christ, and he resisted temptation.

When I wonder what self-control means, I needn't look any further than this: *I call myself "Christian"; I label myself with the name of Jesus.*

"The fruit of the Spirit is . . . self-control"
(Galatians 5:23).

The Fruit of the Spirit Is Self-control

You find faith. You turn your life over to God. You feel clean and forgiven. But how long does that good feeling last?

☞ **Think about it ...**

For most of us, the good feeling of new-found faith lasts until our first big failure—which is to say, the good feeling evaporates all too quickly. What is the missing ingredient that would keep faith strong? Self-control.

Think of those nine qualities God is perfecting in you: love, joy, peace, patience, kindness, goodness, faithfulness, gentleness and self-control (Galatians 5:22–23). We see progress. We have become more loving or more patient. We are more peaceful when things go wrong, and people think us as more kind than we used to be. But just when we think we are on the verge of our greatest progress, we stumble. It is our lack of self-control that trips us up. Discouragement settles in. Faith seems more out of reach than ever before.

Occasionally, we need to stop and remind ourselves that someone greater than us is at work. We will fail. Repeatedly, we will fail. But God has started something, and he's going to complete it. Self-control may come slow. It may seem like we will never shake our impatience. Joy may seem like a joke, and peace unattainable.

We will have our ups and downs. But God will never leave us. He will never abandon the good work he has begun. We will be like Jesus!

☞ **God's Word says ...**

> *"He who began a good work in you will carry it on to completion" (Philippians 1:6).*

☞ **Make it a prayer ...**

> *When discouragement overtakes me, Lord, remind me of your promise to complete the job in me that you have started.*

The Fruit of the Spirit Is Self-control

Perhaps you've noticed: If you have a job to do, and you do noth-ing, little gets done. Do nothing, and you fail.

☞ **Think about it . . .**

The same is true when the job is living your faith. Do nothing, and you will fail.

We like to stress that the job is all God's, but is it? Is that what *he* says? What *is* self-control if it doesn't mean, "I control me?" Self-control is what we need. And that is exactly what it is: *self-control*. It we wait around for some mysterious force to take over, we will have a long wait. It requires discipline to follow Christ. It takes effort. A game plan.

What most often trips you up? What is it that takes your good intentions and shreds them? It might help to make a few notes. Ask yourself: What are my greatest weaknesses? When am I most likely to fall? Is there a pattern? What can I avoid that would improve my chances of spiritual success? Can you become a student of your own life, searching for patterns in your failures and successes?

Discouragements will come, but are you making progress? What do you see when you look back over the past year or two or three? Are you moving toward your goal? Are you taking greater control of yourself than before? Does your character look more like Christ today than it did before? Take encouragement in your progress. Press on!

☞ **God's Word says . . .**

"Continue to work out your salvation with fear and trembling, for it is God who works in you to will and to act according to his good purpose" (Philippians 2:12–13).

☞ **Make it a prayer . . .**

Help me find this place of balance, working out my salvation with diligence, yet knowing that you are working with me, giv-ing me the desire to follow Christ.

The Fruit of the Spirit Is Self-control

When it comes to self-control, how good is our track record? How successful are we?

☞ Think about it ...

How successful are we? Not very. Who doesn't identify with the struggle Paul describes? He painted a picture of a great battle within us. The desire to do good is in conflict with our evil nature. Just when we think we're getting the upper hand, this evil nature asserts itself, and we fall in failure once again.

Self-control begins here, when we face our own weakness. Self-control begins when we admit that we cannot control ourselves. But what happens next? Do we just give up and lower the standards? Some people do.

Instead, Paul pointed to the power of Christ to forgive us ... and forgive us ... and forgive us. But more than forgiveness, Christ would change us from the inside out, little by little, perhaps, but definitely.

Think about your own personal battlefields. Where do you see your greatest weakness? Where do you most need the forgiveness and help of Christ? Is it a problem with anger? Is it a sexual temptation? Jealousy? Gossip? Hatefulness? Can you identify your greatest pitfalls, and turn them into prayer projects today?

☞ God's Word says ...

"I have the desire to do what is good, but I cannot carry it out.... When I want to do good, evil is right there with me" (Romans 7:18, 21).

☞ Make it a prayer ...

Lord, I feel so weak, so incapable to change. I desire to do what is good but falter when I try to carry it out. When I want to do good, evil is right there with me. I need your help, your forgiveness, your wisdom. Without you, I will only fail again and again.

The Fruit of the Spirit Is Self-control

To take hold of faith and claim it as your own is to enter into a mysterious partnership. You link your future to God.

☞ Think about it . . .

In one sense, your life is still yours. But in another sense, you have given it away. You belong to God and have entered into a mysterious partnership with him. You work. He works. You fail. He succeeds. But still you work. And he works.

Self-control means "I control me." Faith requires discipline. It *is* work.

Self-control begins when I see that I cannot control me. My limitations could discourage me. I could lower the standards to ease my guilt. I could walk away from faith. Or I could throw myself into the arms of God.

Self-control happens when I let God control me. It is true, we are in a partnership. Mysterious. Who can understand it? Somehow, God is at work. Even in the middle of temptation, he's creating a door—a passageway that, if I take it, would carry me out and away from the temptation. I do not have to fall. In partnership with Christ, self-control *is* possible. Look back. Recall the last three or four times you failed. Recreate the experience in your mind. Walk through it step-by-step. Do you see the ways of escape? They are there. Keep looking until you see them, then watch for them next time—*before* you fall.

☞ God's Word says . . .

"No temptation has seized you except what is common to man. And God is faithful; he will not let you be tempted beyond what you can bear. But when you are tempted, he will also provide a way out so that you can stand up under it" (1 Corinthians 10:13).

☞ Make it a prayer . . .

Thank you, Lord, for the gift of self-control, for always providing a way of escape.

The Fruit of the Spirit Is Self-control

Through faith, I slap a label on myself: *Christian.* Am I ready to live up to the label?

☞ Think about it . . .

Let's say you put on a shirt. Across the chest, in huge letters, it says, "JESUS IS LORD!" You have labeled yourself. Does it change the way you live? Or if someone notices the shirt and asks about it, do you tell them, "Oh, this? It's just a shirt."

The early Christians thought of themselves as "Followers of the Way." To them, faith was not just something a person *believed*, it was something that had to be *lived*. It was a radically different way of life. To be a "Follower of the Way" was to be a changed person. You could not say, I just believe. You had to *follow*.

Imagine this: Jesus walks up to you and says, "Follow me." Do you respond merely with words: "I believe in you"? Or do you do what he asks? Do you *follow him*?

One day in a city called Antioch, somebody got the idea of calling these people "Christians." You can almost hear it said with a sneer and a laugh. "You people are just a bunch of little 'Christs.' You 'Christians.'" But what could be better than being named after the person you most want to be like? Christian? Sure! Call me a Christian. That is a label I will gladly wear.

Look at that list of characteristics again: love, joy, peace, patience, kindness, goodness, faithfulness, gentleness, and self-control (Galatians 5:22–23). This is the portrait God is painting in your life. It is the image of Christ. Live it!

☞ God's Word says . . .

"The disciples were called Christians first at Antioch"
(Acts 11:26).

☞ Make it a prayer . . .

Thank you, Lord, for giving me the desire to live for you. It is my privilege to wear your label—to believe and to follow you.

Final Words

Each Day, A New Beginning

REMEMBER THIS!

To God, it's not what you do,
it's who you are that counts.

Sometimes we wonder if we will ever change

Long before the sun set, it was hidden from view. Storm clouds rolled in over the Sierra Nevada, the wind picked up, the temperature dropped, and the smell of the coming rain mingled with the scent of pine from the swaying trees. Thunder rumbled and echoed through the mountains. Then, quite abruptly, the skies simply opened, and the rain hammered the earth.

A couple hours later, the wind stopped and the rain abated. Night fell, the clouds parted, the moon rose above the trees and slowly moved among the scattered stars. It was cold.

Twenty feet away, the campfire crackled and spat embers into the night sky. One by one, students stood before that blaze and before the other hundred of us confessed their shortcomings while tossing pine cones on the greedy flames. It was the last night of my first church camp experience, and I had never seen anything quite like it. There were tears of remorse and words of resolve, and I had no reason to question anyone's sincerity.

In fact, later that evening, I stood before my peers, fed the fire, admitted my weakness, and begged God's endurance. I wanted to be a better Christian, and I had said so in words I copied from another sincere camper.

That was Friday. Saturday morning we climbed into our cars and headed down the mountain, trying our best to hang on to those resolutions we made the night before. Unfortunately, my commitment soon faded, long before the memory did.

What keeps faith growing? What is stronger and more effective than the resolutions we make in the heat of emotion? And what can help us break the cycle of discouragement and frustration over our shortcomings?

In the first chapter of this book, I described changes that swept through me "The Summer of My Big Change." Those changes were complete and lasting. But they came a few years after my emotional church-camp experience. What had I discovered in the intervening years? What had I seen in other Christians who were genuinely different and new? What were the ideas that changed me?

Well, that is what we have been exploring together in this book.

To God, it's not what you do, it's who you are that counts.

I had tried to change my life through *doing good things*—going to church, acting religious—or *not doing bad things*. We know about rules and regulations, dos and don'ts. It can be a tiring way to live.

I saw something in Christians who were genuinely different. They had learned a simple, but wonderful idea.

Fall in love with God, and that love will motivate you.

Love, not fear. Love, not guilt. "We love," John said, "because he first loved us" (1 John 4:19). When we see how God feels about us and all he's done for us— when we really believe that—it changes everything.

Christians who are truly new, altogether different, understand something else. They hold on to an incredible idea.

Faith is a dynamic partnership with God.

Remember Paul's words in the book of Philippians: *"Continue to work out your salvation with fear and trembling, for it is God who works in you to will and to act according to his good purpose" (2:12–13).* We work. God works. And in that same New Testament book we have already been assured that God will never give up on us. *"He who began a good work in you will carry it on to completion" (1:6).* Which brings us to another key idea.

We are God's masterpiece in process, and he will not quit on us until he is pleased with the finished product.

"We are God's workmanship," Paul said (Ephesians 2:10). God's fingerprints are all over us. He won't be sidetracked from his craftsmanship, shaping our character. In time, we will be "conformed to the likeness of his Son" (Romans 8:29).

Which brings us back to the purpose and focus of this book. *"The fruit of the Spirit is love, joy, peace, patience, kindness, goodness, faithfulness, gentleness and self-control" (Galatians 5:22–23).* That's what we have considered throughout these pages. But now, as we come to the final few words together, we need a reminder.

Fruit is a product of life.

We have the life of God through faith in Jesus. His Spirit is alive within us! That life, knowing God, will cause fruit to grow. The character of Jesus will sprout and show in how we live. In who we are. "I am the vine," Jesus said; "you are the branches. If a man remains in me and I in him, he will bear much fruit; apart from me you can do nothing" (John 15:5).

We are going to become discouraged at times. We are going to face spiritual failures. The more we love God, the more we will notice them. The more our shortcomings will matter to us. And yet, remember this: Each day is a new beginning. God's love is unconditional. He will not give up on us. Our lives *will change.* People will be amazed. God will be pleased.

This is his concern for you. Because to God, it's not what you do, it's who you are that counts.

Where Do You Go From Here?

My guess is that you care about your faith. To God, it's not what you do, it's who you are that counts—but who you are counts to you too. What you become matters to you. You're concerned enough to read a book about it.

So where do you go from here?

It's important to make time each day to read the Bible, to read it carefully as if it were a personal letter to you from a friend. In fact, that's exactly what it is. You'll find those words will change you. They will make you wiser, kinder, and even, in a sense, happier.

Prayer is also essential. And what is prayer? Conversation with the Creator. God is interested in everything that concerns you. Your frustrations, your successes, your requests, your doubts, your words of gratitude and appreciation and honor, your fears. Your God is concerned about it all, and he welcomes conversation with you. You could think of it this way: When you talk to God, it is a highlight of his day.

Where do you go from here if you want your faith to grow? It's crucial that you spend time with people who value the things you value. Everyone needs encouragement. There are times we would collapse without it. We need the wisdom and viewpoint of other

Christians if our faith is to develop. Faith is not something we do alone; it is something we do in partnership with others. If you are not currently involved in a church, give it a chance. The friendships you establish there could make all the difference in what you become.

One more suggestion: Exercise your mind. Think about your faith. There are books and magazines that will help you understand the Bible, that will strengthen your faith, that will give answers to the tough questions you face. For years, I worked with a publication that was devoted to giving that kind of help. And it still is. Month after month, *Campus Life* magazine tackles the toughest questions about life and faith, and gives honest answers. Love, sex, friendship, loneliness, family, entertainment (even humor)—it's all there. I'm pleased to recommend it, because I know it will help you, as it has helped thousands of other Christians. For more information, you can call 1-800-678-6083.

As I write these last few words, I want you to know that I am praying for those who will read them. For you. Your life matters. God is doing remarkable things in the world, and he's using people like you to do it.

James Long

About the Author

James Long, former editor of *Campus Life* magazine, has won numerous Evangelical Press Association awards for his writing. He has authored eight books, including *Why Is God Silent When We Need Him the Most?* His experience includes evangelism, youth work, and worship ministries. James lives with his family in the Chicago area.

Hooked on the Book
Devotions to Help You Get the Most Out of the Greatest Book Ever Written
Tom Johnson

Get hooked on the Bible? It seems impossible, right? Not so, says Tom Johnson. *In Hooked on the Book*, he helps you discover what the Bible has to say to teens. You'll be amazed at how relevant the Bible is to your life and at what a difference it can make. With stories, humor, and insights, Johnson helps pave your way to greater Bible understanding.

Softcover: 0-310-20499-2

Energizers
Light Devotions to Keep Your Faith Growing
Nate Adams

Daily devotions *can* be fun without being trivial. *Energizers* takes the everyday, sometimes offbeat experiences of real life and uses them to illustrate who God is and how he reveals himself. These fun readings packed with spiritual truth are a great way to energize your daily devotions.

Softcover: 0-310-37371-9

Look for
Hooked on the Book and *Energizers*
at your local Christian bookstore.

ZondervanPublishingHouse
Grand Rapids, Michigan

A Division of HarperCollinsPublishers

Live It!
A Daily Devotional for Students
Becky Tirabassi

Don't just learn about faith—live it! This thirteen-week devotional helps you get serious about following God as it deals with the relationships in your life—to God, to others, and to yourself. Practical and exciting, you won't just live it; you'll love it.

Softcover: 0-310-53751-7

Completely Alive
A Year of Daily Devotions
S. Rickly Christian

Combining two of the most popular teen devotionals ever written—*Alive 1* and *Alive 2*—*Completely Alive* provides a year's worth of exciting, challenging, and encouraging insights into the Bible and how it relates to teenage life. Each devotion gives a Scripture, meditation, and additional Scripture references for further study.

Hardcover: 0-310-20966-8

Look for
Live It! and *Completely Alive*
at your local Christian bookstore.

ZondervanPublishingHouse
Grand Rapids, Michigan

A Division of HarperCollins*Publishers*

We want to hear from you. Please send your comments about this book to us in care of the address below. Thank you.

ZondervanPublishingHouse
Grand Rapids, Michigan 49530
http://www.zondervan.com